A BLUEPRINT FOR YOUR
CASTLE IN THE CLOUDS

D1344203

# A BLUEPRINT FOR YOUR

Barbara Sophia Tammes

make the inside of your head your favorite place to be

# CASTLE IN THE CLOUDS

HAY
HOUSE

HAY HOUSE

Australia • Canada • Hong Kong • India
South Africa • United Kingdom • United States

First published and distributed in the United Kingdom by:
Hay House UK Ltd, 292B Kensal Rd, London W10 5BE. Tel.: (44) 20 8962 1230; Fax: (0) 20 8962 1239.
www.hayhouse.co.uk

Published and distributed in the United States of America by:
Conari Press, an imprint of Red Wheel/Weiser, LLC
665 Third Street, Suite 400, San Francisco, CA 94107
www.redwheelweiser.com

Published and distributed in the Republic of South Africa by:
Hay House SA (Pty), Ltd, PO Box 990, Witkoppen 2068. Tel./Fax: (27) 11 467 8904.
www.hayhouse.co.za

Published and distributed in India by:
Hay House Publishers India, Muskaan Complex, Plot No.3, B-2, Vasant Kunj, New Delhi – 110 070. Tel.: (91) 11 4176 1620; Fax: (91) 11 4176 1630.
www.hayhouse.co.in

Translation: Chantal Loonen

A catalogue record for this book is available from the British Library.

ISBN: 978-1-78180-084-3

Printed and bound in Hong Kong.

for
tommie sophia
and rover

'Change your words into truths
and then change that truth into love...'

*'As' by Stevie Wonder*

# contents

# introduction

All of us could use our very own Castle in the Clouds. A place to retreat. A safe haven where you feel perfectly at home. A place of boundless possibilities where you're in charge of everything and everything is just the way you like it.

The great thing about Castles in the Clouds is that there are no waiting lists. You don't have to apply for a construction permit, get along with the neighbors, obey any laws, deal with hidden defects, or respect zoning restrictions.

We can each have our very own Castle in the Clouds. This time the rich don't have first choice but rather those with a wealth of spirit and imagination.

The foundation of every Castle in the Clouds is based on fantasy. A Castle in the Clouds is created in your head and can be as large and as detailed as you can imagine. If you like the idea of drawing your own Castle in the Clouds, feel free to do so. It's a great excuse to buy yourself a pretty journal or sketchbook. This same book can be used to note the answers to some of the questions that come up as we design our castles, but that's up to you. And if you are one of those people with a tendency to want to do everything the right way—then don't. That's not what this is all about. You don't have to finish your homework or give the right answer to every question. What you come up with today may be different tomorrow. What seems like the right answer today can contradict itself tomorrow.

It is best to save space for change, for doubt. And unlike in your real house, you never have to finish the construction of your Castle in the Clouds.

Basically, you'll be redecorating the inside of your head. It's a kind of mental architecture, or true interior design, you might say. You can create space for everything that's inside of you, giving it a beautiful setting of its own. Your imagination can build a magnificent Castle in the Clouds, like an inner oasis of twenty-five mind-expanding rooms (three prefab castles, twenty rooms, a garden, and stables) that offer a mild look at yourself. Your castle is a playground for self-discovery and the sweetest place to meet with yourself.

> Your Castle in the Clouds is a place to imagine yourself into happiness. Using your imagination feels good in itself. It offers a chance to disappear for a while.
> But imagination also has the power to transform reality and redesign our sense of self, so that we can emerge renewed.

The inside of your head should be your favorite place in the world. Make it beautiful. Decorate it with illuminating ideas, clarifying insights, and loving thoughts. Just use your imagination.

Building Castles in the Clouds is one of those things that children do much better than those of us who have been living this life a bit longer. So the sooner you start, the better. You really can learn to use your imagination again, to think funny and beautiful thoughts—just for the fun of it! You can also use your imagination to serve a higher purpose. Step out of your everyday life, with all its rules and restrictions, and dream up new possibilities. Discover what your true desires would be if there were no limitations. Then have the courage to place those desires back in the reality of this life. Try it and see how much you can accomplish. The path to new realities runs through the imagination. If you can't even imagine and visualize the kind of future you want, how could you ever hope to make it happen?

As long as your thinking remains bounded by rules, laws, and restrictions, you'll never stretch reality. But if you can manage to express your true desires in words, experience them in images, sense them in scents, and feel them as emotions, then you'll be able to change paradigms and create a new reality. Call it a wish-fulfilling prophecy. It's similar to a self-fulfilling prophecy: if you're sure something isn't going to work, then you're probably right, and the opposite is equally true. By focusing on your desires rather than your fears, you improve your chances of steering reality in the right direction, and you set yourself up for success. Later in life, when you're supposed to be grown up, fantasies are considered a waste of time. Instead, everyone talks about how focus is what we need. The funny thing about focus, though, is that it's really nothing more than a stubborn, persistent fantasy. Focus is a fantasy that grips you by the throat and won't let go, no matter how hard you squirm.

The more you use your imagination, the better the odds that your fantasies will take root and turn into focus. And don't forget that having an idea is still the best motivation to get out of bed in the morning.

You picture yourself in the near future with hair blowing in the wind galloping a big jet-black stallion through beautiful valleys while you are actually going around in ever-repeating lame circles on an old horse called Muffin trying to grasp the basics of riding.

You picture yourself this evening at a beautifully set table surrounded by all your friends with radiant smiles on their faces, while at this very moment you're lugging your groceries and then trying to keep yourself

> Everything starts with imagination. Imagination is the source, the food, the rocket fuel for focus—and quite possibly for everything you do.

This handbook sparks your imagination with a catalogue of everything you might want inside your castle. It explains how to start building and what questions can reveal your true desires. It encourages you to make choices by giving you plenty of options. Think of it as the Sears reflex: if there's a page of vacuum cleaners in front of you, you automatically start to pick one out, even if you don't need one and hate vacuuming. When you have choices, it's only natural to choose.

from grabbing hold of the cashier to drag her over the conveyer belt because she is tossing everything into an egg-crushing heap past the cash register.

So give your imagination plenty of space. The older you get, the more you may tend to believe in the laws and rules and boundaries that people have made for one another. You may start to think that your boss can tell you how much you're worth by deciding whether or not to give you a raise. Or that love is measured by how much praise you're getting—or think you're getting. Or that being invited to that trendy party means you must be pretty fashionable yourself. Before you know it, you've given other people control over your reality.

This is why building your Castle in the Clouds helps you take control and be who you dream of being. You can now begin putting your energy not into fighting reality but instead into looking at it from a new perspective. The perspective from miles above, in the safest, most wonderful wish-fulfilled place you can imagine, is where you're free to be your highest self. View the perspective from your very own Castle in the Clouds; then look back down at your old reality.

You see, sometimes you have to believe it before you can see it.

This handbook helps raise your imagination to a new plane by providing design suggestions for a variety of mind-expanding rooms. Think about how different you feel the moment you walk into a church or a museum. Rooms can shape your mood.

So go ahead and indulge your boundless, endless, materialistic cravings: take, want, desire more. Give yourself everything you deserve, everything you've lacked, and more. Towers, ballrooms, waterfalls, private white sand beaches, and more. You don't have to worry about debts or about buying the wrong thing. You don't have to feel guilty, because this time you can only grow richer.

> Imagination is the kick start to reality.

# tools

To start building, you have to create space in your head, be open to fantasizing, mentally stretch to erect an elaborate Castle in the Clouds. Time seems to be essential for creating space, but the intensity of your thoughts is far more vital. To give your full attention to your Castle in the Clouds, it is important to be relaxed. And don't make too much fuss out of being relaxed: if it doesn't seem to work, just pretend. Don't force yourself, fool yourself into relaxation.

## RELAX

A walk in nature is relaxing. An endless massage is extremely relaxing. That is pretty obvious; I mean, if you have the time, everything can be relaxing, even frying an egg. But let's assume, just for the fun of it, that you don't have the extra time.

Relaxing can become difficult, especially when you are stressed. To tell someone to relax is just as ridiculous as advising someone who's afraid of dogs not to be

Don't force yourself, fool yourself into relaxation.

afraid—or to make matters worse and tell them dogs can sense their fear. Must relax = stress = the opposite of relaxation. So don't. Just forget it.

Just pretend that you are completely relaxed. Visualize yourself in a complete state of serenity. Just imagine that you are. Start with your body, and the rest will follow. It's true! Eventually your head will buy into it. Don't force yourself, just fool yourself.

The physical signs of a relaxed body are calm breathing, soft muscles, and a controlled reaction.

## BREATH

Start with your breath. It is very calm when you are relaxed. Pretend to have a calm breath. A calm breath is slower: slow inhalations and even slower exhalations. Start by pretending that you are exhaling very, very slowly. Your breathing not only quiets, it feels easier too. If you were relaxed, your breath would be low, from the belly. Pretend to breathe from the belly by expanding it on every inhalation and pulling it back in on every exhalation. Sit up straight as if there's a string attached to the crown of your head that's pulling you up.

Drop your shoulders down and give more space to your rib cage. Think slow inhalation and just a bit slower exhalation—and in between a moment of total nothingness.

## MUSCLES

Pretend as if your eyes are softening. If you were truly relaxed, your mouth and jaw would feel loose. Pretend by opening your mouth a tiny bit, letting your lips just be. Tickle the roof of your mouth with your tongue; it might make you yawn. Press your tongue lightly against the roof of your mouth so you can be sure you can't clench your jaws together.

Drop those shoulders, you don't need ear warmers. Imagine your hands feeling warm and soft. Everything hangs loose.

Try to imagine how every molecule in your body is carrying itself. Every molecule is in its own place and is strong enough to carry its own weight. It is exactly where it is meant to be. Not one single molecule leans on, pushes, or pulls another.

## REACTION

Forbid your body to react mindlessly. You haven't ceded control over your surroundings or whatever is happening or could happen, but from now on you're just pretending not to pass any impulsive signals on to your body. Oops, sorry, you just forgot.

So when your two kids in the backseat are trying to get at each other, you can hear it, you can see it in the rearview mirror, you could say something if you want, but you're just going to pretend that it is not registering in your body. No red spots in the neck, no short, high breaths, no urge to turn around to whack

wildly in their direction. Just concentrate on your body. You're observing the reactions and guiding them from there. Slowly inhale, exhale just a little slower.

So if a colleague at work takes credit for your efforts and tries to put you in a bad light (pretty clever by the way), you know this is unjust and will do whatever is within your power to get your own back, but your body does not participate; it does not get riled up, it continues to observe. Your head may go nuts, but you just pretend that your body hasn't noticed. You don't let it affect your breathing, and you don't move a muscle. Continue to breathe slowly, to open your mouth by pushing your tongue against the roof, to lower your shoulders. This will automatically create an emotional distance that will give you a wider perspective.

Guiding your reactions is usually the hardest part. It is advisable for starting DIYs to pick a quiet place and time. Once the foundation of your inner castle is solid, you will be able to visit even for a brief five minutes while the world around you continues at the same breakneck speed. Just take a moment in your (still to be imagined) golden primal spring bath.

If you don't succeed in relaxing, don't get stressed about it. Keep those shoulders cramped against your ears, let your eyes jump out of their sockets because you have to keep an eye on everything. Instead, just express your desire. So don't say: "It's not working, it's not working, I'm still stressed," but express in a heartfelt way (which doesn't have to be out loud, it can be somewhere in your head), "Oh how I would love to be relaxed." Sigh. Start again.

in    out

Here you go. This is the key to your Castle in the Clouds.
Please sign to show you've received it and that you agree to the terms.
To be really good at fantasizing, you need to let go of rational constraints.
You can do that by signing here.

Yes, I give myself permission to fantasize without a goal—uselessly, carelessly, without compromise, and endlessly childishly—about things that could have been, about things that will never happen but feel pretty and pleasant, about things the way I want them to be.

Yes, I give myself permission to make the inside of my head my favorite place to be.

DATE                     PLACE                     SIGNATURE

# pre-fab castles in the clouds

To start you off, here are three prefab turnkey Castles in the Clouds for you. You can stay in one of these while you are building your own Castle in the Clouds. Once your own castle is done, you could still use these as a holiday home—just because it can be nice that somebody else has imagined everything for you. Feel free to make any personal adjustments you like.

## 1. BEACH HOUSE

The beach house is a solitary house on a private piece of shoreline in a secluded bay. It is made from driftwood.

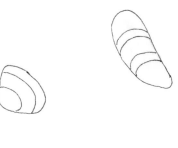

In front of the house is a table with an assortment of chairs found washed ashore at the beach. Next to this are bricks built up in the shape of a horseshoe where you can build a fire or barbecue. The front of the house has a porch, and every pillar is the trunk of a different tree. You made wind chimes out of shells, and they are hanging from what's left of the branches of those trees. On the left side of the porch is a faded orange hammock.

In the middle is the door frame with a fly curtain made from shells and little pieces of driftwood. Once inside there are two wicker chairs on the left. A Spanish guitar leans against the wall. There's a large wooden bowl on the table filled with perfectly sun-ripened fruits bursting with juice. A small counter is built against the far wall. A refrigerator underneath is filled with transparent bottles with the finest pure springwater. On the right is an enormous bed made up in fresh, white linen sheets, large pillows, and a spacious mosquito net. Next to the bed is a little lamp made from an ostrich egg with pinholes in it. When the light is on, it creates little stars on the wall. Behind the bed, in the right-hand wall there is a large window with wooden shutters. In the corner is a large open shower with beautiful Moroccan tiles.

It is lovely and cool inside, with a sensual breeze moving through.
The wooden floor feels soft and warm and is worn smooth by all the bare feet walking through. It smells of sea, wind, salt, sun, and freshly burnt wood from outside.

When you walk in, your body feels supple, strong, and healthy. Your warm bare feet feel free and pretty. Because there's no need here for tightly fitting shoes, your toes are slightly parted, and your nails are naturally white (or a prettily colored polish).

You feel sensual and relaxed, attractive, sexy, full of life, slow (due to sea air) but not sluggish. You are grounded on both legs with your feet deep in the warm sand. This gives you a feeling of trust and internal safety.
Your skin seems to be your most important organ. You can feel the warmth of the sun, the wind that moves the little hairs on your arms, the softness of a T-shirt you wear at the end of the day, the sand between your toes.

Your body is in a state of complete relaxation, but strong. Your muscles feel powerful yet supple. You feel beautiful; your hair is glossy and your eyes are shiny.

Imagine standing underneath the shower while the fresh water beats down on you with a strong but pleasant force. You are eating a large nectarine. You bite into the skin—it's hard enough to offer a bit of resistance—and the juice runs over your chin but is instantly washed away by the running shower.

You moisturize your body from head to toe with a luscious, silky cream. Try to imagine how you rub it into every little part of your body.
Try to get a good idea of how a healthy body feels. Feel the fluid power in your muscles. Feel the lightness of every molecule in your body that carries it's own weight, doesn't push against any others, and has its own unique place.

Think of who you would like to be with you. Fantasize about the things you could be doing.

> The Beach House can be used to imagine having a body that doesn't feel tight or blocked anywhere. This enables you to let all the energy and feelings flow freely through you in a body that surrounds you completely and fits perfectly, so you don't try to get away from it and escape into your head. How would your body lead your life if it was up to him or her?

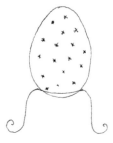

## 2. TEA PAVILION

The pavilion is a well-preserved octagonal Victorian building, with windows all around. It was built in 1900. It's part of a large estate, with a mansion, a carriage house, and a boathouse. You can't see the other buildings through the trees, but sometimes, when the wind blows from a certain direction, you can hear the sound of people's laughter in the distance. These people could be your family, friends, friendly acquaintances, or friendly unknowns who have the potential to become your family or friends. Someday.

The pavilion is on an open sunny spot on a lightly slanting lawn. It smells of freshly cut grass, oxygen, spring air, and a subtle hint of roses.

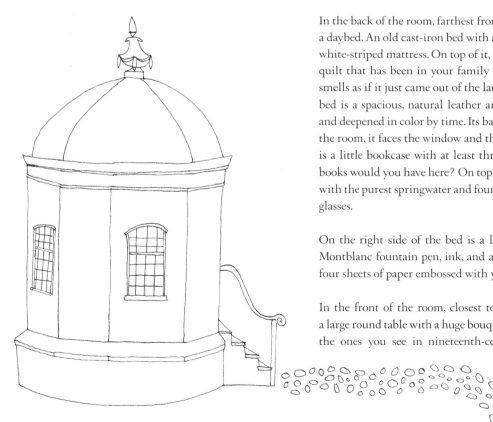

You are walking on a path of smooth white pebbles, so big that they feel comfortable underneath bare feet. The path winds through the green grass and ends at the entrance to the pavilion.

The front of the Tea Pavilion has a small porch with four steps leading up to it. The wooden handrail feels smooth because of the well-maintained paintwork. The wooden steps are a bit worn in the middle, so pay attention when you walk up the steps. The wooden doors with little panes of glass open easily, and you find yourself in a large stately room with light entering from all sides. The floor is a brightly polished oak. You can hear the sound of the birds, a soft breeze, and a solo cello playing beautiful classical music.

In the back of the room, farthest from the entrance, is a daybed. An old cast-iron bed with a thick, blue-and-white-striped mattress. On top of it, neatly folded, is a quilt that has been in your family for centuries but smells as if it just came out of the laundry. Left of the bed is a spacious, natural leather armchair, softened and deepened in color by time. Its back turned toward the room, it faces the window and the view. Next to it is a little bookcase with at least three books. Which books would you have here? On top of it is a decanter with the purest springwater and four stemmed crystal glasses.

On the right side of the bed is a little desk with a Montblanc fountain pen, ink, and a stack of twenty-four sheets of paper embossed with your initials.

In the front of the room, closest to the entrance, is a large round table with a huge bouquet of flowers like the ones you see in nineteenth-century paintings.

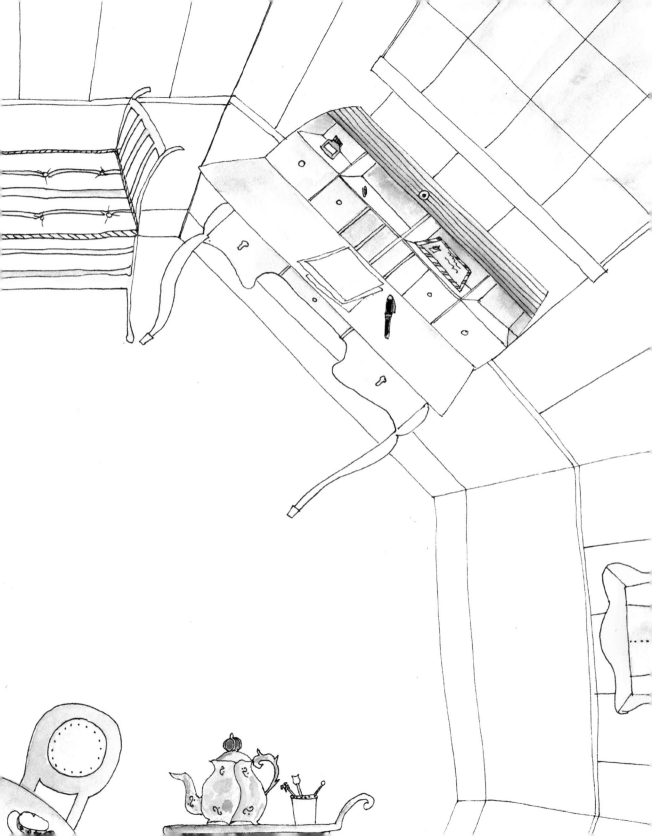

A lot of them are still waiting to open. They smell more of a promise than of the sometimes overpowering scent that goes with a bouquet in full bloom. There are two chairs by the table. The velvet upholstery of one is pale green; the other, pale blue.

Next to it is a butler tray on wheels with an old Chinese porcelain teapot and four matching cups and saucers. One of the cups has a tiny chip, and when your lip touches it, it feels like a funny little dent. In an old silver baby cup with your name on it are three silver teaspoons. One with the crest of the place where you were born, one with the first letter of your first name, and the other with a little silver horse.

On the left wall is a portrait of an old male ancestor, and on the opposite wall a portrait of an old female ancestor. You never knew them, but when you look at them, it is as if you recognize them. You feel comfortable being here.

It all feels easy on the eyes.
When you enter this place, your body feels clean. Your head is clear and fresh. You're sharp, not only can you think clearly, but you can put those clear thoughts into clear words. You walk with a straight back. Your breathing is calm. Your eyes are wide open. You are rested, totally present and alert, with calm expectations. The stately room gives you a natural sense of peace and authority, a noble feeling of distance from people, things, business, and problems. This provides you with a useful perspective on the things happening around you. The corners of your mouth are slightly curled up; there's a little mischievous sparkle in your eyes. Your natural state of being is amused.

When someone asks you a question, you give, after a brief moment of rest, a sharp and witty answer without raising your voice. You are free of fear, you feel no anger: this is no place for extreme emotions.

You are wide open, but the world does not touch you; alert, but not suspicious.

You can use the Tea Pavilion to imagine yourself in a dignified and calm state. How would you deal with the things that wind you up in daily life and occupy you for an unnaturally long time? Imagine that you have invited the person you clash with the most into the Tea Pavilion. What will your conversations be like when you are in this state?

## 3. TREE HUT

In an ancient forest stands a century-old oak tree. A Tree Hut was built high up and safely embraced by its long branches. Stairs with twenty-one steps circle up around the trunk and end by a porch. Once you are on the veranda, there is a breathtaking view of an endless sea of branches and leaves. There's a rocking chair on this porch with a brown cashmere blanket with fringed ends hanging over its backrest.

You can hear the murmur of the wind and the rustling of thousands of leaves.

In the middle of the Tree Hut is a wooden door with a little heart cutout. When you open the door, you enter one general space. Everything is made out of wood, and you can smell the different types: cedar, pine, rosewood. In the middle of the room, the tree rises up through the ceiling.

All four walls have windows with wooden shutters. There's a large wood-burning stove, and it's comfortably warm. On the stove is a large round-bellied kettle and an enamel coffeepot. There's a thick, warm rug on the floor, made from dark brown woolly sheepskins. In front of the stove is a chair covered with a sheepskin, a hassock is on the floor, made of wool. There is a large bunch of flowers on the table with eucalyptus and a few deep red amaryllises.

On the floor, leaning against the wall is a chessboard. The light and dark squares are worn from use.
To the right of the entrance is a cupboard bed. Its wooden doors, also with cutout hearts, are open. Inside is a thick mattress and a stack of thick, soft blankets, and a large, soft pillow of freshly washed cotton. From the wooden ceiling hangs a little oil lamp. A little shelf at the foot of the bed contains a few books.

When you enter this space, you can feel clearly that you are part of something bigger—lifted and heightened, safe and protected, wise, closer to heaven, in touch with nature. Because of the grandeur and beauty around you, you can't help but feel a deep respect for all that lives, including yourself. When you are in the Tree Hut, you feel rich and grateful for everything you have and are a part of.

It seems like your breathing slows down and adjusts to the rhythm of nature, of the rustling of the leaves. Your inner voice calms down, and your heart beats slower, like that of a bear in hibernation. Your head is switched on, refreshed, and in a sparkling meditative state. You feel as if you are a thousand years old, as old as the tree itself, and as if you have lived through it all three times before.

Your soft-natured, mild, nonjudgmental self, who is definitely there inside of you, gets a chance to come out here. That is because you are completely secure here so you can feel safe.

Because of the silence, you feel even closer and more connected to your surroundings. In this state of rest you can experience a sense of bliss.

The Tree Hut can be used to imagine being in a state of higher consciousness. By imagining, experiencing, tasting, smelling, breathing and feeling it, you're practically there. By wishing: I would like to feel the connection to a larger whole, you are opening yourself up to it.

decorate the inside of your head
with fresh new ideas,
positive thoughts,
fun memories,
and loads of love.
keep it open, fresh,
and clean as you
would do with your
favorite space.

true interior design

The prefab Castles in the Clouds—the Beach House, the Tea Pavilion, and the Tree Hut—can be added to your own Castle in the Clouds. In fact, there are no rules for your Castle in the Clouds.

You can add floors and give those a special meaning. You could place your highest-valued rooms on the upper floors, for example.

You can choose your own colors and scents, the structure and its architecture. You can have anything whether that's a pink Barbie palace, a Gaudi variation, or a simple shack.

Next you will find specific rooms offering different possibilities, for you to use or to change and adjust to your own wishes.

You can start anywhere you like. You don't have to think about supporting walls or anything technical. You don't have to finish the room, and you may dwell in it that way forever.

Take ten deep, calm breaths and count them one by one, while imagining taking ten steps. Your first decision: are they taking you up, higher into the sky, or down, descending deeper within yourself? It's up to you—or down in to you, for that matter.

1

2

3

4

5

6

7

8

9

10

Before you start decorating your rooms, you may want to think about how you would like it to smell in your Castle in the Clouds.

of sleep

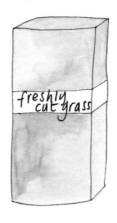

freshly cut grass

freshly washed and wind-dried white shirt

of oxygen

of a clean freshly hayed stable

of vanilla

of sun of skin at the end of the day

of freshly washed love

an open-air wood fire

of rain in the forest

of a new book

of a well-oiled saddle

of clean sheets

following your nose

of cinnamon buns

of warm, melted butter on freshly baked bread

of cappuccino and the ink of the Sunday paper

of warm milk on the breath of a sleeping baby

# Salon

Your social skills dwell in the Salon. This is where you are at
your most beautiful, your brightest, your finest, your
sharpest. You could easily perform a play by Oscar Wilde in
your Salon. You have a smart, witty, yet charming answer to
everything. Utterly civilized. You feel awake, alert and sharp,
yet relaxed. Your eyes have a little twinkle, and your body
feels silky smooth.

You are surrounded by things of beauty. What do you see?

## THE TROPHIES CABINET

Imagine a cabinet of trophies in the Salon. This cabinet could house everything that symbolizes what you are proud of. There are five polished golden cups with brass plaques on the pedestals. What's engraved on them? It could be a challenge you won, be it a physical or a mental one; it could be something you overcame, some goal you reached, an achievement. It can be a wise decision you once made. It can be the best compliment someone has ever given you.

Only you can decide what is worth a trophy, because only you know the effort it took. Some days getting upin the morning is a huge achievement or not getting into an argument or swallowing your pride. Overcoming silly fears—wearing a new shade of eye shadow, being firm with the sweet lady at the store, having lunch by yourself, saying no to, well, just about anyone—can all be more than good enough reasons to be engraved in brass and stuck on a shiny cup.

You don't have to justify any of the trophies to anyone but yourself. Do what you think is best.

To help you make a start, you can present five cups to yourself for:
1. A fear you overcame
2. A good decision you've made
3. Something you've accomplished/established/an achievement
4. The most unique aspect of your character
5. A treasured compliment someone gave you

The cups are there for all to see. And you certainly don't have to stick to five; there are hundreds at your disposal. The more you have, the better you feel; you just have to be able to remember them all. Good for you if you can. Give yourself a bonus cup for being so generous to yourself! That is one swell quality.

Here are your trophies. What does it say on the plaques?

You will be interviewed by Oprah Winfrey shortly. You are sharing tea in your finest china, and you get to have a sneak preview of the questions she will ask. What are you going to say? Give your coolest answers—this is no time for false modesty.

- How did you become who you are now?
- What could people learn from you?
- Were you this special when you were a child?
- How did you cope with the setbacks in your life?
- What can we expect from you in the future?
- Which actress/actor should play you?
- What actor/actress would match well with you?
- Which well-known song could be about you?
- Who has been in love with you?

- Who could be in love with you if they would only get to know you?
- Could you tell me more about your five trophies?
  - How did you overcome this fear?
  - How did you come to this decision?
  - What challenges or obstacles did you have to overcome to achieve this?
  - What makes this trait so unique to you?
  - Why did this compliment touch you so deeply?

Oprah ends the interview by saying: "I'm happy I had the chance to get to know you better. I admire you. Thank you for being so open." She turns to the camera and informs the audience of the next topic. You don't hear any of it, you are glowing in a warm dream state. You have been seen and heard and have been greatly appreciated for who you are. That was about time.

The Salon
is a great place to take time to appreciate yourself. Well, it's actually far more than that: to glorify yourself. This is a room where you can be proud of yourself for all the big and small things you have accomplished, a place where you fearlessly radiate confidence and provide an open invitation to anyone around you to do the same.

kitchen

You can go to your inner Kitchen when daily life is bombarding you with impulses and information. This is a place where you can think about what you do or don't want to consume or digest. It's like when a remark is aimed at your head but resonates in your stomach. Instead of an immediate reaction, you could take that remark to the Kitchen and decide if you want to stew it for a while before you consume it.

The Kitchen could occupy a central place in your inner castle. In the Kitchen it's always warm and cozy, it smells good, and it's a good place to be yourself. This is where your deepest hunger is filled, leaving you completely satisfied—not sluggish and full-bellied, but satiated and content. This could be a good basic state of being. You are nurtured, physically, mentally, emotionally, spiritually, and can handle the greatest adventures. You are truly, fully satisfied, and it's a good way to start just as it is a good way to end the day. You are open to everybody and everything; anything can happen and it is perfectly all right if nothing happens. You're in neutral—a perfectly peaceful state of rest.

## FEEDING THE BODY

In addition to food, exercise is an essential need of the body. Movement. Don't design your Kitchen too small, nothing is better for dancing on than a kitchen floor. Nobody is watching, nobody expects anything. To get into the basic state of rest, you could have a good dance. Do some stupid dancing, offbeat dancing, weird dancing, shame dancing, pretty dancing, small dancing, extravagant dancing, dirty dancing—anything—as long as you do a bit of moving to music in some sort of rhythm.

Dance the way your parents dance, penguins dance, a sheep who wants a good shearing. Dance like a filly on her first day in the field, like a moth who's attracted to the fire, like a lady. Dance as a Native American or a shy Rasta. Dance, dance, dance.

## A HEALTHY DIET

Your body is perfectly capable of teaching you what is or isn't good for you. Your body is not stupid and won't eat anything that smells or looks spoiled. If you do put something that tastes bad into your mouth by mistake, you spit it out. You could treat information, impulses, or remarks in a similar way. Who says you have to swallow everything? Who says you have to take it all in? If it's hard to digest, you shouldn't consume it. If your piece of bread is moldy, you don't go after the baker; you just throw it away. Do you think you could do the same with cruel remarks, manipulative compliments, and double-edged jokes that make you feel uncomfortable?

Try to decide, just like your body does, if you want to take it in. If you swallowed something by mistake that you would have preferred not to, give yourself time to digest it.

You could make use of the special oven in your Kitchen. As with food, you could heat up people's remarks a little to make them less tough. This old-fashioned Aga stove has four ovens: a stewing oven at the bottom left, a cooking oven top left, a baking oven bottom right, and, the hottest, a roasting oven top right. Decide which oven you should place the remark in. If it is just a little nasty, put it in the stewing oven for a while and then decide if you still

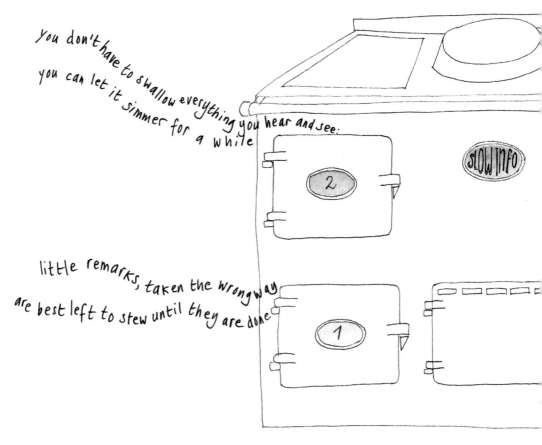

You don't have to swallow everything you hear and see. you can let it simmer for a while

SLOW INFO

little remarks, taken the wrong way are best left to stew until they are done

want to "eat" it. A deeply painful remark can go in the hottest roasting oven, hellfire. After a while you could check, see if you feel like it, will it taste okay? If it doesn't, don't have it, just leave it in there until it burns to a cinder. If someone aims a remark at you, it doesn't mean you have to accept it. It's like a gift—just like food. You just say, "Thanks, but no thanks."

By putting a moment of consideration in between a remark or piece of information and the moment you decide to accept it, you take full responsibility for the care of your well-being. You create a moment of choice. You can't choose what people will say to you, but you can choose whether to swallow it or not.

The Kitchen can be used to nourish yourself with information and thoughts that are good for your well-being. Your inner Aga is an aid, a simple rating system, to help you become more aware of what information gives you energy and what information takes your energy.

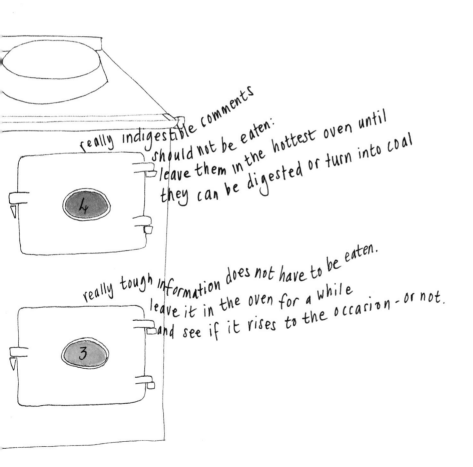

really indigestible comments
should not be eaten:
leave them in the hottest oven until
they can be digested or turn into coal

really tough information does not have to be eaten.
leave it in the oven for a while
and see if it rises to the occasion - or not.

You can choose not to consume
certain information or input,
just like you can consciously
choose to nourish your mind with
beautiful words and thoughts.
Which cup of tea could you use now?

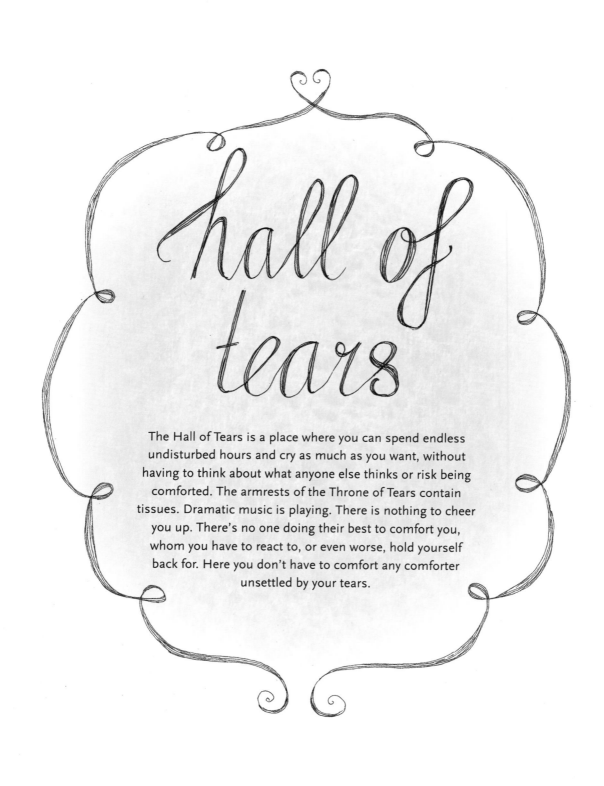

# hall of tears

The Hall of Tears is a place where you can spend endless undisturbed hours and cry as much as you want, without having to think about what anyone else thinks or risk being comforted. The armrests of the Throne of Tears contain tissues. Dramatic music is playing. There is nothing to cheer you up. There's no one doing their best to comfort you, whom you have to react to, or even worse, hold yourself back for. Here you don't have to comfort any comforter unsettled by your tears.

In the Hall of Tears your tears are caught in little bottles, labeled with the name of your sorrow so you can find them to cry all over again next time. It shows you all the things that made you sad before in case you need to cry some more.

Not everybody is good at crying. You could be afraid that you will never be able to stop. And let's face it, some sadness is just too much to even get started on. Just know that sadness is universal. So you may want to choose to delegate some of your sadness to professionals; they cry for all the suffering in the world and they will be happy to take yours too. Watch and learn how crying should be done—not the pitiful blubbering you try to get away with sometimes, but rather the wailing, with buckets full of tears and snot. Someone else's pity is even better than self-pity.

You know there's an absolute finite amount of tears that has to be shed for each sorrow. For a big sorrow it is nice to have some people to share the crying with you—or you could be crying for the rest of your life and still have tears left over. So take your pick of one of our professionals, and let them get a head start on the crying. Or ask them to finish the job when you are too tired to cry any longer. You could even hire the entire thousand snotty members of the Saliva Army, who will cry endless tears for you. How many people will have to cry and for how long? How many tears is this sorrow worth? Only you can say.

You can go for quantity to help you get over your sorrow, but you could also imagine a specific person for this job. Who could lighten your heart by taking on a part of the necessary crying? Think of who you would like to assist you in crying over your pain.

Which bottles of sorrow are in your Hall of Tears?
Did you reach your absolute finite quota in tears?
Or should you add more tears?

*Get somebody else to cry for you when you feel it's getting to be too much:*

## GAIA

Gaia is like a huge, endlessly flowing waterfall with an infinite source of tears for all the children and loved ones she has lost. Gaia feels all motherly sufferings. She understands you completely and will cry as many tears, full of love and understanding, as you want her to shed. You could ask for her help for short intensive periods when she cries exclusively for your pain, or you could immerse yourself in the world's suffering and have her cry 24/7, so your tears can slowly trickle away within the flood of those of the rest of the world.

~ gaia ~

~ virginia ~

## VIRGINIA

For the tears you think you're not entitled to, Virginia is our expert on mixed and confusing sorrow.

It's possible that the sorrow you're involved with is not made up of pure sadness, but also is part anger. Even if the suffering is not pure sorrow, the tears that have to be shed are. Virginia has so much empathy that she can distill and shed the purest tears for you even in the cloudiest case of pain, sadness, jealousy, confusion, shame, or numbness. Included in the service is a crystal bottle to catch those tears, so you can save them to remind you—and maybe even to prove—how much sorrow there really is.

> Get somebody else to
> cry for you when it's
> just too much. Pick one
> of our professionals.

~marina~

## MARINA

No matter how deep you dig, you never hit water.

Marina is especially for people who can't cry, not even when they imagine being in the Hall of Tears. Marina holds an ocean of tears for every sorrow. Just because you are not capable of crying, it doesn't mean you don't know pain or sorrow.

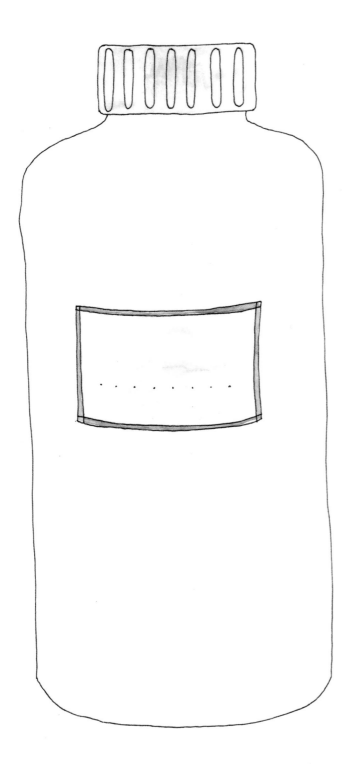

What is your biggest sorrow?
Have you given it all your tears?

The Hall of Tears can
be used to inventory your sorrows.
Every sorrow holds an absolute finite
amount of tears that will need to be shed—by
you or by somebody else—without comfort or
sentiment. And at times you may discover that a
particular situation is not that bad. You might not want
to admit it to the rest of the world and you don't have to.
(You may be secretly relieved that that old smelly dog
finally kicked the bucket, but you don't have to tell
anyone—ever.) Then there could be other sorrows
you are not done with even if the rest of the
world doesn't understand. (That you still miss
that silly, smelly dog, but you don't have
to tell anybody about that
either.)

On the next page,
you can pick labels
for your bottles
of tears.

for friendships
without
a future

for the
person
you no
longer are

for joy

for being touched

for that
time your
heart was
broken

for who
you will never be

for all those
times you were
misunderstood

for the time
you broke
someone's
heart

for the
memory of
your mother's
soft hands

for
beautiful
fading
memories

because
everything
passes

for all the
times you
held back

for
losing trust

because it's
impossible to
live on without
you

for that you
wish you hadn't
done

for you

for losing faith

because you end up alone anyway

for injustice

because it is hard to accept that life goes on without you

for what they should never have done

for bad timing

because it could have been different

for all the inconceivable suffering in the world

for sorrow that wears off

for everything that failed

because it sucks

for the memory of your father's generous smile (or the absence of that smile)

for all the memories you would have liked to have had

{ for me }

for all the times you weren't true to yourself

for everything you didn't do

# mental spa

You can design a Mental Spa in your Castle to clean disturbing and limiting thoughts off of the inside of your head, just like you shampoo the outside of your head.

In the bathroom of your real home, you wash yourself using shower gel, you treat your hair with shampoo and conditioner, and after drying yourself with your towel, you put some fancy cream on your face. Then, you spray a little bit of perfume on yourself. (And by the way, who's going to explain to all the young men that a little spray is not the same as a barricade of Calvin Klein anyway?) Only then do you feel and look nice and clean.

But meanwhile, inside your freshly groomed head, mothy, rusty, false, and sly thoughts are generating themselves; they seem to be budding in the roof of your mind. That is why you need to expand your Castle with a Mental Spa to clean the inside of your head—to wipe away the disturbing, limiting, destructive nonsense in there, and get a truly fresh and attractive head this time, inside and outside, instead of a gleaming l'oreal coupe that seems to look good but hides terrible thoughts.

You need this Mental Spa, so that, while you get a manicure, a mask, and hot stones on your back, you can also work away all the irregularities in your mind.

## FRESH AIR

Before whipping up this mental beauty treatment, you will need to identify which thoughts are disturbing you. And therein lies the big challenge. You've probably come to think they're part of you—something that never goes away. Maybe you are these thoughts. And that'll make it really hard to get rid of them.

What could be of help to you is to picture these thoughts as if they're birds—twittering birds. And just like birds, they come along and fly on by just like that. The trick is not to try to catch them, but rather to let them fly by.

You don't get angry at birds when you see them outside your window. Likewise, you don't have to get angry at all the thoughts that come flitting by. It's fine for the thoughts to be there, as long as you don't try to hold on to them, or even worse, identify with them. Just remember: you're not what you think.

You don't have to take responsibility for your thoughts. Any bird could fly into your head. In other words, any thought could come to your mind, depending on what's going on around you. You're free to think anything, but those thoughts really don't say much about you. At most, they tell you something about your imagination, your fascinations, or your frustrations right at that moment, but they don't say who you really are. It can be reassuring to keep that in mind. You don't have to account for each and every thought, only for what you do or say because of them.

There are many types of intrusive thoughts. Like an ornithologist out in the field, you need to learn to identify and name them. To what species do they belong? If you know that, it's easier to keep them from polluting your mind. It's a kind of mental hygiene. Take your time and try to cleanse yourself. Lie in a hot bath, wash your hair, do whatever you want, but also try to flex your back and think on which birds have been flying through your head. Recognize them and let them go—without being judgmental.

When thoughts fly by, put tags around their legs, so that you can recognize them later. Try keeping track of the thoughts you notice in the course of a day or a week. And feel free to come up with your own species beyond those listed here.

# species of birds

## THE CALL BIRD

Call birds are tempting thoughts that try to distract you when you're in the middle of something. "I wonder what's on TV? . . . Why don't I check out the H&M website? . . . Have my Facebook friends already commented on my new status?" Hear them out, recognize them, label them, and let them go. Call Birds love it when you lose your train of thought. It's in their nature. Still, just flying by is fine by them too.

## THE MOCKINGBIRD

Mockingbirds are self-sabotaging thoughts, destructive mantras like "You're too fat. . . . You're too thin. . . . You're no good at this anyway. . . . It's too late now. . . . Who cares? . . . You're a real disappointment. . . . You're being ridiculous again." and even "Who do you think you are?"

You could fill a book with all the different varieties of Mockingbirds, but their most important characteristic is that they make fun of you, and not in a constructive way. Their jokes aren't funny; they aren't even supposed to be. They are pure waste, poisoning your mind.

The Mockingbird is a very common species and can survive under the most varied and bizarre circumstances. Mockingbirds can find something to taunt you with in any situation. So don't be surprised if you notice them flying by more often than you might have expected. Learn to identify them, tag them, and let them go.

callbird

appealing thoughts that distract you

mockingbird

sarcasm and self-mockery that undermines your confidence

## THE DIPPER

Dippers are repetitive thoughts that make you feel sad, like "Nobody loves me.... I don't love anybody.... I'm not worthy of love.... People are bad by nature." They may repeat things your parents or teachers might once have said that are still echoing in your head. Dippers are thoughts repeated over and over again that have become solid convictions.

Dippers are a hardy species, related to Mockingbirds. The biggest difference is that Dipper thoughts can easily be mistaken for your own inner voice. These are the thoughts that often remain unspoken. And, since no one has the chance to contradict them, they often appear to be true.

Dippers disguise themselves as deep insights, dark secrets, and dismal truths. You can identify them by their call. They don't twitter or chirp; instead, their plaintive coo sounds like it's coming from the depths of your soul. It is often followed by the thought, "How awful, but that's just the way it is," or, "As long as nobody ever finds out."

The Mockingbird is obviously not very constructive, Dippers, however, can be mistaken for the truth. They're not quite as common, but they're harder to get rid of and leave a trail of destruction wherever they go.

Try to recognize Dippers for what they are. Here's a good rule of thumb: a thought is a Dipper if it makes you feel deeply unhappy and you can't be 100 percent certain it's true (and that is often).

Thoughts of fear and anxiety may be seen as a Dipper's eggs. If you give them attention and start to breed them, they easily become full-grown convictions.

Recognizing the Dipper for what it is, a sad projection that you have come to believe, is a huge achievement.

## THE HOUSE SPARROW

You may notice humdrum little thoughts that keep popping up in your mind. We call this type of thought a common House Sparrow. Its song is fairly dull and ordinary: it keeps repeating all the things you still have to do. This little sparrow may seem harmless enough, but it can eventually lead to panic. As its call repeats again and again, you may start to think your head is full of sparrows. What you need to do is identify this bird, tag it, and recognize that it's just one Sparrow, calling out to you over and over again. When you have thoughts like this, make sure not to let them add up. If you remember five times that you have to pay a bill, that doesn't mean you have to pay five times, even though that's often how it feels. Recognize the Sparrows, and say to it, "I've already seen you. You're the same one!" Then let it fly away.

Some House Sparrows repeat bigger worries and fears, and it's this constant repetition that makes them candidates for the Mental Spa. Just pay attention to the Sparrow's call, and set a time to face that problem.

### dipper
an unpleasant thought about yourself
that has become a conviction

### house sparrow
listing all the things you have to
do or worries on your mind

## THE PARROT

Parrots are uninvited thoughts that mimic what other people have said, or could have said, or might have thought. Parrots fill your head with irritating squawks: "When she said, 'Shouldn't you be working?' what did she mean? Does she think I'm not working now? Does she think I don't like working? Does she think I work too hard? Does she think I don't work hard enough?"

The same principle that applies to your own thoughts also applies to other people's. It doesn't matter what people think, because we're all free to think whatever comes into our heads. So respect the freedom of the people around you, and respond to what they say and do, rather than to what you think they may be thinking.

Your own thoughts will keep you busy enough as it is, don't pollute your head even more by latching on to what others might think.

## THE CUCKOO

Cuckoos are always calling out their own name. The Cuckoo in your head does this because it's awfully impressed with itself (and you) and doesn't have much interest in anything else. Whenever anyone tells a story, the Cuckoo draws a connection to itself and has a hard time letting the other person finish. The Cuckoo distracts you while you're listening and wants you to talk about your experiences, your opinions, or anything else relating to YOU, YOU, YOU. If you were looking for an excuse, you could call it enthusiasm.

The clever Cuckoo can be pretty devious and give you a question to ask, so that it looks like you're interested in what the other person is saying. But it's really just a way of steering the conversation back to you, you, you. The Cuckoo is bit of a nasty bird who comes to spoil your beautiful hairdo and your reflective mind-do by popping up and distracting you with ego babble. Scare him off with a loud, hissing noise. And then, open yourself up and listen to others again.

parrot

repeating what other people could
have said or might have thought

cuckoo

bringing every conversation
back around to yourself

## THE WOODPECKER

The Woodpecker flies around in your head constantly hammering out its arguments. With every peck it defends its view of the problem. Unfortunately this makes the problem more important than the solution. The Woodpecker keeps repeating to you that something another person did was stupid, unfriendly, rude, thoughtless, or just plain wrong. As it hammers away at what seems like the winning argument, it actually stands in the way of a solution—and above all, it stands in your way.

When there's a Woodpecker in your head, you might wonder why it feels so important to be in the right. Sometimes you want to be right because you want permission from yourself and the people around you to get angry, to set limits, or to feel whatever it is you actually feel. (To put it simply, when you fall and nobody appears to feel sorry for you, there is less satisfaction in crying.) In fact you're the only person who can decide what hurts or offends you and what doesn't. So there is something very peculiar about the Woodpecker and its arguments. You don't need permission to believe what you believe, or to feel what you feel. There will always be someone who sees things differently. So don't go pecking up the wrong tree.

In short, the Woodpecker is the argument that pops into your head and gets stuck on repeat. If you can identify it, you can treat it as the waste of mental energy it is.

## THE POORWILL

The soft, pitiful cry of the Poorwill tells you how badly you've been treated, how unfortunate your situation is, and how difficult it has been for you. The difference between the Poorwill and the Dipper is that the Poorwill likes to show itself, while the Dipper pretends it doesn't exist and passes off its cries as your true feelings.

Just like children who refuse to wash their hands or don't want to take a bath, you may sometimes feel reluctant to let go of this bird.
It's time to be strict with yourself and force the issue.

Wash your hands before dinner, visit your Mental Spa once again before an important meeting, and get rid of this pest.

woodpecker

hammering away at arguments to convince or defeat imaginary conversation partners

poorwill

softly whining about how hard life is for you

## THE BIRD OF PASSAGE

The Bird of Passage is a thought that loves to escape—almost a thoughtless thought. But to escape, you have to come up with all sorts of excuses: "That's not for me. I'll do that later. I don't need this. Thanks, I'll pass," but the Bird of Passage sometimes tries to negotiate: "I'll stop tomorrow," or, "Five minutes is enough. It's better than nothing." Unlike Mockingbirds, which enjoy coming out in the open, Birds of Passage don't like to be spotted. This is a big difference and can help you to tell the two species apart, even though they look similar and often work together. The nervous Bird of Passage hides behind the attention-grabbing Mockingbird.

## THE EAGLE

The Eagle flies high above it all, observing the whole landscape with its sharp eyes. And the Eagle in your head always has an opinion. It constantly compares, connects, and tries to understand the bigger picture. This Eagle is a very smart bird and can actually be quite helpful, as long it comes and goes at your invitation. But if its stream of commentary never stops, it soon becomes a nuisance. Sometimes, it's nice to experience things without a story, a plan, or an agenda. There's plenty of time for words and thoughts later.

As you drive down a street, the Eagle asks, "Would I like living here?" Right away, it starts assessing and comparing, but it forgets to smell the magnolias. The Eagle gives you a detailed description of whom you are dealing with, the moment you are introduced to somebody. So if you listen to this bird, you may never truly see them.

### bird of passage
always trying to escape

### eagle
the keen-eyed commentator who has
to learn to keep quiet sometimes

## TIME FOR A BIG CLEANUP!

Cleaning out your mind is actually very simple. You don't need to scrub it hard, you don't need expensive creams and elixirs, you just need to detect and get rid of those vile ideas that trouble your thinking. Poof, leave them between the discarded cotton pads in the bin.

You can release disturbing thoughts bird-by-bird each time, but you can also ask yourself which ones flew in a few times a day, and "open the cage" to release them all at once. That is what mental hygiene is all about.

## BIRDS OF PARADISE

There are also pleasant thoughts that you could welcome into your mind. Let's call them Birds of Paradise. When all the other birds fall silent, you can hear them as they soar through your head, saying things that are funny, beautiful, or kind. When your life is repeating itself, you often stop noticing Birds of Paradise. But when you look at your everyday activities with fresh eyes, you invite Birds of Paradise to say sweet and silly things to you.

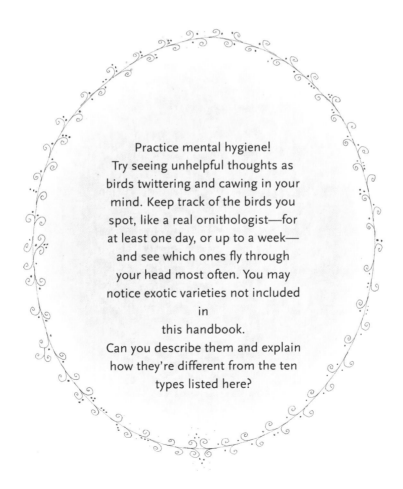

Practice mental hygiene!
Try seeing unhelpful thoughts as birds twittering and cawing in your mind. Keep track of the birds you spot, like a real ornithologist—for at least one day, or up to a week—and see which ones fly through your head most often. You may notice exotic varieties not included in
this handbook.
Can you describe them and explain how they're different from the ten types listed here?

## SUSTAINABLE WASTE MANAGEMENT

You can recycle the waste from your Mental Spa! In other words, you can teach your birds new habits: not completely different habits—they'll never do your groceries for you or wring out your wet socks—but you can put their natural characteristics to work for you. You don't have to silence them; instead, you can change their tune.

For instance, the Call Bird can help you concentrate by luring you back to the task at hand. "Hey, your mind's wandering again," it might say to you.

If you're taking yourself too seriously, the Mockingbird can help you see the funny side. It says: "Try laughing at yourself. It works for me."

Now and then you can ask the Dipper to sing to you about your deepest desires. It knows all about them, since they're often the flip side of your greatest fears. And ask the Dipper to use its sense of drama. It will love you for it.

You can ask the House Sparrow to dictate a to-do list, when you have a pen and a piece of paper ready

You can teach the Parrot to respond to all of your theories and suppositions with, "Is that so?" All day long: "Is that so?" Every time you assume something is true: "Is that so?"

You can give the Woodpecker an affirmation to hammer away at. He'll be very grateful.

You can ask the Cuckoo to help you take good care of yourself, by repeating YOU, YOU, YOU whenever you're treating yourself with contempt or neglect.

You can teach the Bird of Passage to say, "Either do it now, or quit talking about it."

Once in a while, let the Poorwill express itself for a while. For once, give yourself permission to believe every word. Have a self-pity party in front of the TV, or wherever you like.

The Eagle is a very important bird: his call is most like your own true voice. Ask the Eagle's opinion at those times when you're prepared to truly listen.

> You can install a Mental Spa in your Castle in the Clouds to help you to become aware of intrusive and limiting thoughts and to learn to flush them away regularly.

# head office

If you feel lousy or confused, there is a good chance your inner secretary has filed your experiences and accompanying emotions in the wrong folder. Here is some good advice: fire your secretary right away and take back control of your inner Head Office.

## FIRE YOUR SECRETARY

Why do people always tend to react in the same way? Why does one person always get angry when something happens, and another is always overcome by guilt? Why do you usually react in a similar way? It's because you've got a lazy secretary in your head who files every event and every experience you have in the same folder, always. Out of habit. And you have never confronted her about that.

To start with, fire her at once, without notice. Don't feel sorry for her; she'll find a new head in no time. There are plenty of vacancies in the head department. Then start to experiment with filing these events and the feelings that go with them yourself. Humor yourself and label things a different way; see how that feels. How does it feel if you file a failed attempt at something in the DESIRE file instead of the GUILT file: the desire to get it right next time.

The feeling of guilt costs as much energy as the energy delivered by the desire to do it right.

## FILES

Your secretary's work is not that hard. You'll get the hang of it in no time. There are three types of files: red, green, and yellow.

The red files contain all the emotions and feelings that surround a particular event or situation. Every feeling gets its own folder. Some may be brand-new as they have never been used. The green files are for the action you should take. The yellow ones are eventually used to save the event. Experiment with feelings. There are emotions that overcome you and there are emotions you can summon, and both can be transformed into a feeling, experience, or lesson of your own choice.

Something happens in your life. An incident. The automatic secretary is ready to put it in the "POOR ME" file once again. After years of experience she knows you will feel this way. And yes, she's right, if you label it like that, that's exactly how it feels. Spot-on. If you didn't know better, you'd think you had a brilliant secretary. How on earth is it possible someone knows you so well?

While your old secretary is gone and you are looking for a new one to replace her, you could do your own filing for a while. Experiment with feelings. There are emotions that come over you, there are feelings you can tap into, and both can be transformed into the feeling, experience, or lesson you choose yourself.

For example, you can put any situation in more than one red folder, because every event has more than one feeling. A lover breaks up with you—always a hard one.

First, you put it in the ANGER file, because you are angry. It's not the breakup itself, but "the way it was done"—you know the drill, all those things you say to yourself and a lot to others. Then you become sad. Put it in the SADNESS folder. You miss your lover, the fun stuff you used to do together, and all the things you were going to do. That makes you upset again. Back into the ANGER file. Then see what happens if you put it in the FEAR folder. What are you afraid of now that it's over between you? And how much of it is a hurt ego? You could find out about that by putting it in PRIDE. Go back to SADNESS: is it waning, is it clarifying? Then you file it in DESIRE, the desire for things to work out with the next lover, version 2.0. Once you have recalled, relived, and tried out every feeling surrounding an incident, a rationalization will take place, followed by an action. Choose the right green folder, maybe more than one. When you feel sad, you need to cry. Put it in the CRY file. The green folders are for the action you need to take. It sounds logical, but it hardly ever goes smoothly.

Once you've cried, gotten angry, and done everything else you need to do to transform the released energy, you can start to think about how to save this event in a yellow file. How would you like this experience to fit in with the rest of your life? What did it bring you? Is it still a part of you? This lover was so crude but you want to avoid making that same mistake twice, so you save it in the WISE LESSONS file. Or all things taken into consideration, it makes a great story and can be saved in BEAUTIFUL MEMORIES. Or you never want to think about it ever again, and you put it in TRASH.

## INSTRUCTIONS FOR THE NEW SECRETARY —YOU!

### TAPPING INTO FEELINGS

First, you raise every single feeling that a situation can come up with. You can do this by refiling it in different red folders to save it under a different label each time. That is what you do: rename it over and over again. Gather all the energy that will be released by intensely living and feeling the situation. How much anger, desire, fear, etc., are you feeling?

Ask yourself the questions: What if I were to get angry in this situation—What or whom am I angry with? How angry am I? How would that make me feel? Do the same with every conceivable emotion. Give it time. Some emotions need more time than others. Sometimes you need to let it simmer or blow on it like on a smoldering fire that could turn into a raging inferno. Rather than putting the brakes on, give it some more fuel. What could make me really sad in this situation? Unleash the drama queen. Give her a stage and a microphone. It's all happening in the safety of your own mind, inside your own inner castle walls, so let it rip.

The more energy you can get from all the emotions that just happen to you, the more powerful the transformation can be into a feeling of your own choice.

Now grab an old file of something in your life that made an impression on you or confused you—maybe it still does—and do the work your secretary should have done. Take the experience out of its folder like a cold case and tap into it as if it's happening now. Run it through all the files and see what you can make of it this time.

### THE RED FILES

#### ANGER
What is it about this situation that is making you angry?

Anger is rage. Rage can be felt all over, especially in your limbs: you just have to move them. You may remember this feeling from when you were a young child. Anger can be felt when things do not go according to your plan. That's why it happens more often when we are young, when all day long we have to do things we didn't choose and we don't understand the necessity for or see the point of. Because rage goes hand in hand with stomping toddlers, we try to give it a different name in adult life: "I'm disappointed." "I just need some space for a while." If anger is not expressed, it can backfire within and turn into depression. There's nothing wrong with being angry. It just doesn't always have to be put in action. Acknowledging those things you are angry about can be an enormous relief. Don't forget that this is not the stage where your feelings have to be justified. That has nothing to do with it right now. The sole purpose of the secretary is to take an inventory of those things that are alive within you.

Anger can be useful if it leads you into action. So question it again: What makes you furious? What makes you outrageously mad? What pisses you off more than anything? Don't be surprised if sorrow appears once you have admitted to yourself that you are very, very angry. Allowing the anger to be what it is releases a stream of other emotions.

> Remember that it's the secretary's purpose to take an inventory and file. It's not her job, and now is not the time, to condone or condemn these feelings or to have any opinion on them at all.

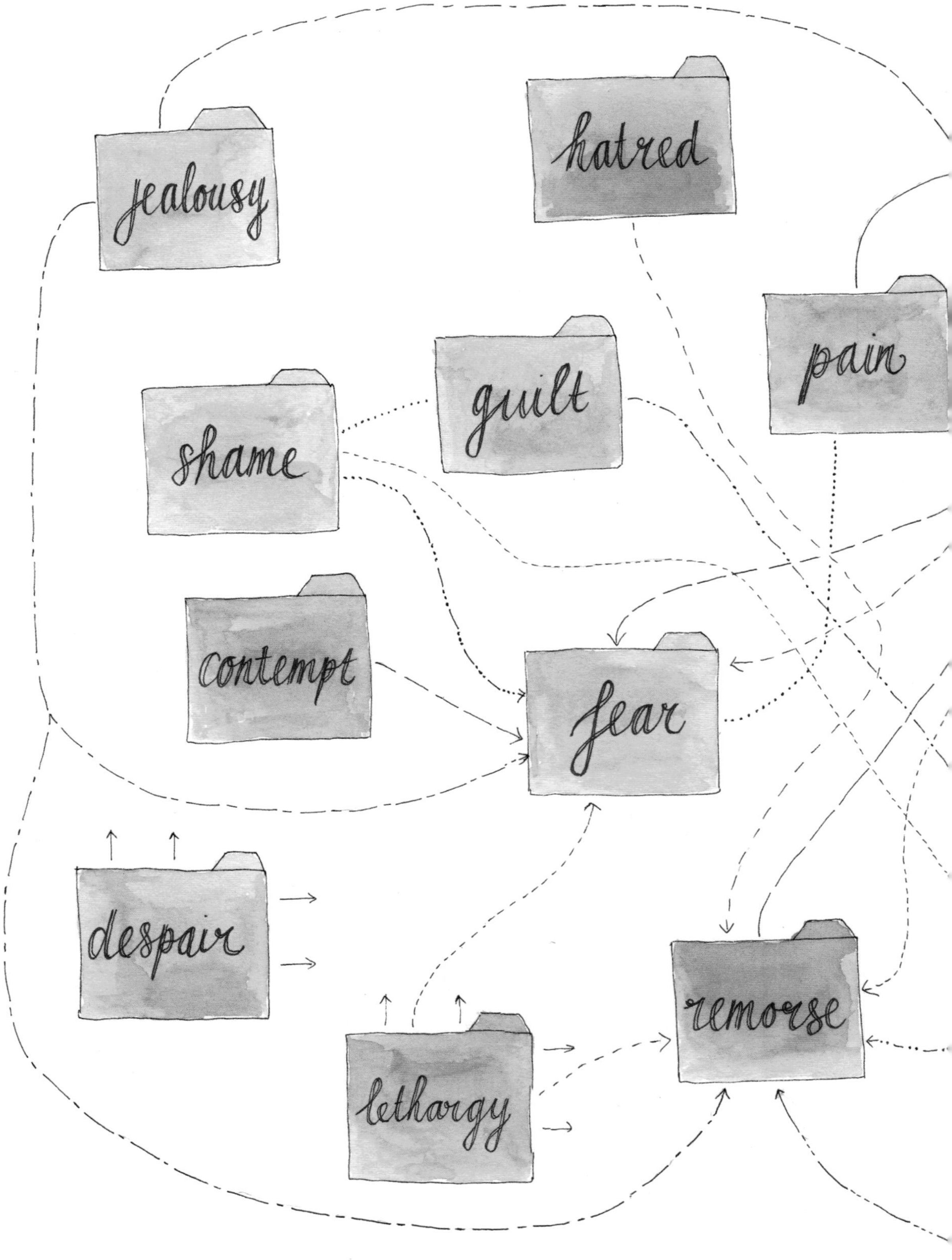
jealousy
hatred
pain
guilt
shame
contempt
fear
despair
lethargy
remorse

pride

decisive-ness

gratitude

excitement

sorrow

action

desire

love

sweet memories

wise lessons

anger

Your feelings are guided by
the name you give them.
Different label = different feeling.

## FEAR

What are you afraid of? What are you afraid to see? What scares you to even think about?

Fear grabs hold of you so tight you're stuck. You can't move or breathe properly anymore. Fear can be about physical things: fear of drowning, fear for lack of sleep, fear of not performing well enough. And there are mental fears: fear of not being seen, not being loved, not being good enough. Fear can be justified, which makes it very useful, and fear can be unjustified, meaning there is work to do. You can leave the fear in the folder if you can be 100 percent sure that it's true, i.e., you aren't good enough and you will drown. In any other case, you must lift the paralysis by staying in motion. What else is going on?

Fear can be subtracted to expose other pure emotions. Fear will often try to come back to you, but try not to dwell on it for too long. Feel the fear, acknowledge it, and move on to another folder.

## DESIRE

What would you wish for if anything were possible? And what do you wish for within your means?

Pure, undiluted desire is a wonderful feeling you can invite in in large quantities. Desiring something new doesn't diminish what you already have. Desire doesn't mean less when it's never fulfilled. Desire opens doors, space, and freedom to all kinds of possibilities. The more desire you have the courage to express, the more chances you have to shift those rusted frameworks and old paradigms and expand your reality. Desire is pure oxygen for the future.

Desire is the nemesis of fear: overcome fear by feeding desire; let the desire to do something grow bigger than the fear that'll stop you from doing it.

Try to see, in clear pictures, how you want a situation to be. And check if that really is what you want. Walk around in it, experience your desire. Desire is a powerful catalyst that comes before faith, which is needed to make real changes. Actually, desire can over rule reality and even operate without faith because it is so strong, huge, and powerful in its own right. Feed your desires into enormous proportions.

## SORROW

What makes you sad?

Sorrow can feel pretty good. It is the overwhelming proof that you are capable of giving and feeling love for something, someone, or some situation. Where sorrow is pure, it cleanses. To make sure that your sorrow is pure, go through all your files and remove anger and fear. What's left are pure tears. Let them flow, don't hold back.

## PRIDE

What makes you proud? Has you pride been hurt or damaged?

Pride can be a noble thing in itself. Pride makes you that little bit taller. It gives you the courage to use more space. You can breathe in more air. But pride also has a petty downside. When ego experiences a shortcoming, that can hurt its pride. And here's a paradox for you: when ego finds itself on the wrong side of pride, it is too proud to admit it. Try and keep this file clean/pure, for noble pride only. Hurt pride is fear, and it's misplaced in this folder. Noble pride is a great way to move into desire and feeling decisive.

## EXCITEMENT

Is there anything about this situation that gives you energy?

When you feel excitement, your breath moves up in your chest and you're almost holding it, your blood tingles, and you can't sit still. Try and get as many situations into this folder, that is, after you've extracted the anger and lived through that. Excitement is the battery, and you can choose to run it on love, desire, and noble pride.

## JEALOUSY
### Is there anything you would like too, something someone else has and you don't (yet)?

Jealousy is a very old emotion. You've known it since childhood. Some people know it better than others. If you stay on the right side of jealousy, it can even be a compliment and make you feel good—the fact that it is possible that someone wins the lottery three times in a row, that it's possible to fall head over heels in love at seventy, that it's possible to sell a simple idea for a lot of money. If you can see it as proof of the endless possibilities in life, you can swiftly move it into the desire file and wish it for yourself too. If you begrudge the other person and find it worse that someone does have that when you don't, you're on the resentment side of jealousy. If it hurts a little and it seems to go in the direction of resentment, you might want to experiment with fear and anger a bit more.

## DESPAIR
### Does it look like there's no solution?

Despair is a tough one. Despair feels endlessly dark, heavy, and low. It's a bit like lethargy. It stops everything. Try to stay in motion. Use lots of folders. Try to find out if you are truly desperate. Or are you afraid the solution might not work? Or are you afraid to get mad at the person you hold equally responsible for this situation? Do you think you could sneakily dare to have the desire for a good ending?

## LOVE
### Can you still feel love in this situation?

Love feels big, spacious, and all-embracing, and it can be focused on something minute. Love makes the corners of your lips curl up; you can slowly breathe an enormous amount of air into your body that spreads without any obstacles. Keep coming back to this file even when you think the situation has nothing to do with it. Try every time to squeeze a little love out of it.

## REMORSE
### Do you feel remorse?

Remorse feels reasonably calm, a little sad but not too complicated. Feeling remorse is taking full responsibility for what happened and accepting it without a fight. It's more of an ambiguous feeling of "I wish I had handled that differently or hadn't done it at all." Remorse cleanses. After a reasonable period of remorse, you should be able to move it straight into the desire file (to never do this again), then into a green or even straight into a yellow folder.

## HATRED
### Do you feel a deep hatred?

Hatred feels good and bad at the same time. The power of hatred feels pretty good, as if you could actually do something about the situation. You are not a victim, no one messes around with you, there will be justice at last. However, holding on to hatred paralyzes you. Hatred needs constant motivation. Hatred is hungry and wants to be fed by a certain idea of reality that justifies itself. "That neighbor is really stupid, my God, how stupid can a person be? Look at what a stupid thing he's done this time!" Motivation is the weakest link of hatred. The justification is the killer: either you are right, something bad was done to you and the constant repetition of the event will hurt you, or you are not entirely right and your hatred is just too big. Your intrinsic universal sense of justice gets all tangled up. To keep your hatred in place in that situation means you have to rehash that small part of the story where you may have a point. ("Okay, so he's very nice to his wife, children, and the rest of the neighborhood, but have you ever seen how he pulls on his dog's leash when he takes it for a walk … ?!") It's exhausting and not very constructive. You are selling others and most definitely yourself short that way. The Woodpecker is a close accomplice of hatred. Hatred does have the function that it sends out a signal, so if it's there, take inventory and label it. Hatred is often a desire to be extremely angry.

When you get out of hatred's path and allow yourself to be angry, because you give yourself permission or pluck up the courage to do so, you'll often find that the sorrow file presents itself. Feeling hatred appears to feel safer than anger. Being angry is something you have to learn, it will get you a lot further than hatred. And hatred could be camouflaging fear.

So don't try to jump from hatred to love in one leap, that's nonsense. Observe what's left of hatred once it's passed anger, despair, fear, and contempt. And try the odd gratitude every once in a while as well.

## SHAME
Is there anything you are ashamed of?

Shame feels kind of dirty. Shame gets into your clothes, your hair, your breath, your house. Shame is a tough one. You want to hide shame. Shame congests. A lot of events tend to get moldy in the shame file. Best not to look at it in the hope it will disappear, wear out, or be forgotten. But as long as it stays in that folder without exposure to oxygen, it will not disappear. You have to actively move it into another folder. Try fear, guilt, or remorse.

## GUILT
Are you feeling guilty about something?

Guilt is a gnawing feeling. You sense it in your gut. You want to push it away, but it keeps coming up. Guilt is remorse + self-destructive anger, which becomes clearer when you separate the two. Take the anger file out and get very angry with yourself for a while; then you can get the remorse file out and feel what it's really all about.

## CONTEMPT
Are you disgusted with anyone who had something to do with the event? Do you look down on someone? Is there someone you consider a lesser person than yourself?

This is something you usually find out when you're trying to prove a point to others. You need others to agree that this other person is indeed lame/stupid/a moron. Contempt is hard to admit, but it can cause obstructions in a big way. So it's not a bad idea to at least admit it to yourself. You can catch yourself when you like to say bad things or gossip about that person. Contempt is often just fear, fear of being like that person you despise. If you were to be 100 percent sure that you are not in any way like this person, your contempt would lose its grip. So if you feel contempt, move it back into the fear folder for a while. Why is it so bad to be like this person? Then you can move it into the decisiveness file and promise yourself you will never be anything like this person.

## DECISIVENESS
What are you able to change?

Decisiveness feels good; it's like a brand-new day when everything is possible. Once you remove the anger, it is a very constructive emotion. If you come here from the desire file, there's a big chance you will succeed.

## LETHARGY
Are you not feeling anything?

Lethargy is anger and being powerless turned inward. It is a bit too easy to just advise you to just let the anger out. While your feelings are in this file, you would be wisest to shift and refile and shift some more. Keep trying all your options open until you are given a clue where to start.

## PAIN
Do you feel pain?

Pain is like a stab that makes you contract; it feels overwhelming. Pain is like a zipped computer file: it's easier to send, but in order to really feel it, you will have to unzip it. Pain is a composed/compiled feeling. Unzipping it is achieved by putting it in different files in order to find out what's there. Or, in case you are computer illiterate (by the way, isn't it about time you fixed that?) in different words pain is a container concept, it can be a combination of a whole lot of other feelings. Try exploring the files for fear, anger, and sorrow to untangle the pain.

## GRATITUDE

What is the lesson here? What are the good things about it? What did this situation make you see? What could you be grateful for?

Gratitude is a very fulfilling feeling. It is a deep steady feeling that grounds you and lifts you up at the same time. It excites you and relaxes you simultaneously. You can derive gratitude out of almost any other feeling. Sorrow can make you feel alive, anger can open up doors, shame can indicate what's important to you—that is if you don't get stuck in these files but move on to the gratitude folder. Gratitude has a direct connection with bliss and can be directed at the tiniest shiny raindrop on a new green leaf as easily as at life-changing events like a baby being born.

Gratitude is the bonus that comes with growing older, when there is cumulatively more to be grateful for. Keep placing the gratitude folder on top of your stack to keep reminding yourself of what you can be grateful for. Of course, some days that is harder work than on other days. But hard work is nothing to be scared of.

## THE GREEN FILES

Once you have summoned all the emotional content for an event, you can use this energy to transform the feeling around it into a feeling that does help you or that you have chosen. This is called rationalization.

Secretaries tend to start with the green folders—with action. They try to control your emotions by skipping them. You can get angry over and over again, or cry all the time, but it won't help because you are not solving the actual problem. You're going around in circles. You can't file it neatly. It keeps coming back.

In that case you go back to the red files. It seems like it takes up a lot of time, but it saves time in the end.

The emotions of the red files are universal and can therefore be explained. The actions that need to follow in order to feel better, meaning the green files, are personal and depend on the situation. The right red file will usually lead to a singular action ready to be undertaken. You can trust in that. Here are a few examples, but think about the things that will help you.

For instance:

## CRY

When there's sorrow, you should cry. Softly and small, hard and copious, often and sometimes. It may sound silly to even say it, but so often we forget to cry.

## BE ANGRY

If the event keeps coming back to the anger file, there comes a time when you have to get angry. And acting out anger is scary. This is because most people are not very good at it. Not being angry, we are pretty good at that, but expressing anger is an art form. Dosing anger is the hard part. Either you are afraid of becoming too angry, or you've expressed your anger in such a neatly and fluffily packaged way that it didn't hit the spot. There are special courses you can take with the anger managers at the Royal Suite of Evil for that.

## PROTECT

Think of how to protect yourself or the other person. What do you need to feel safe?

## VISUALIZE

Try to imagine how you want a situation to be—in a practical and realistic way, down to the smallest detail. Fantasize; feel the desire. What does this teach you?

## PLAN

Make plans on how to achieve what you really want.

## DREAM

Dreams are desires without consequences. Dreaming is being where you want to be for a little while.

## ACCEPT

Sometimes you have to give up a desire. If and when you have assured yourself that a certain path is truly impossible (you want to marry Mick Jagger), the time has come to accept it. It's much easier to do so when you have tried every which way to make a go of it.

## LOVE

Can you love things as they are? Including yourself?

## LEARN

Learn what is needed to achieve your goal.

## FORGIVE

Disengage your feelings from the people who you think did this to you. Don't deny the feeling, the feeling is yours, but the people may have had different intentions.

## DISSECT

Take the situation apart and break it into smaller pieces that you are able to handle or understand.

## DISCIPLINE

The solution to almost everything is that you have to come up with a system of rules that you stick to. "I can't check his Facebook page again" or "I will stop gossiping, because it makes me feel bad every time." Choose a framework that feels safe to you.

## SET BOUNDARIES

Think of how you do and don't want things. Practice the words and expressing them.

## IGNORE

Forget it. What were we talking about? Can't remember. Whoosh. Gone.

## GIVE IT TIME

Give yourself the guarantee that all will be well, let it go and give it some time.

## TAKE CARE

Stroke, take care, comfort, cuddle, cocoon, caress, bathe, pamper yourself.

## APOLOGIZE

You don't have to be completely wrong to apologize. You could apologize to yourself. Apologizing is a way to acknowledge what happened AND a promise that it won't happen again.

## SAY YOU'RE SORRY

You can say you're sorry without offering an apology. "I'm sorry things didn't work out between us." You are only trying to say you feel it's a pity things went the way they did. It's pretty subtle. A lot of people like to hear a confession of guilt in it though.

## CLEAR UP

Clean your house, empty the kitchen cabinets, go through your mail, get rid of old clothes. Hopefully you'll end up with a clear mind as well. This is a good solution to a lot of things.

## LAUGH

Take your fun seriously. Do things that make you laugh and take your mind off of things you are dwelling on. Dance, sing, run around, make fun of yourself, paint, build a bonfire, swim—whatever comes to mind. You know it is true, so just go do it now.

## THE YELLOW FILES

Finally, when the situation has been experienced and it is over, you can decide where and how you want to store it. You can choose one of the yellow files or even to trash it. This is in fact an answer to the question of how you do want this or don't want this to influence your life. It actually tells you who you want to be.

The stronger your emotions, the more power and energy they have to transform into feelings of your own choice. Pick among the yellow files and the trash for storage.

SWEET MEMORIES

WISE LESSONS

NO LONGER A PART OF ME/TRASH

You can choose to remain alert by active filing instead of keeping the automatic pilot on. But now that you know the ropes, you might consider hiring a new secretary. Here are a few applicants.

> The Head Office can be designed to disengage the automatic pilot from your thinking and to allow you to make your own choices on what you want to feel and how to label those feelings.

## THE WARM SECRETARY— MISS BEAULAH

Miss Beaulah is forgiving, and she loves you. She wants what's best for you, and she wants you to feel good. She's very honest and actually wants everybody to feel good. When you are angry at someone, she will ask you if you could be afraid of something. And let's be honest: what are you afraid of? She will put every event that you are angry about into the fear folder first, to take the fear out of the anger and see how much anger is left after that. Most often, it's not a lot.

## THE PRACTICAL SECRETARY— MISS HANNAH

Fear is a very practical emotion. Fear is a survival mechanism. When you are afraid, the adrenaline in your blood increases, your breathing accelerates, and you receive more oxygen. This heightens your alertness and ability to react—often what's needed in new (scary) situations. So it's good to be afraid. Don't look at fear as a signal to stop, but use the excitement to move on and be thankful for the extra power it gives your body to master this scary/new/fearful situation. That's Miss Hannah's reasoning. She files almost everything you are afraid of in the excitement file.

## THE DUAL JOB—
## MISS PUCK & MISS PIPPAH

Puck and Pippah have a rather philosophical nature. They share one job and confer about everything. Everything has its reason and lessons. Right? What one has filed neatly, the other can take out and put in a different file just as easily. They advocate a roller coaster of feelings. Everything is to be experienced and reexperienced—and bowled over again—until it all quiets down.

## THE COOL SECRETARY—
## MISS SAVANNAH

She is of the opinion that everything can be traced back to one emotion—from anger about not being loved enough to fear about not being loved enough to desire that you will be loved enough. That's how Savannah thinks—everything is desire. But that seems so hard to control. Sometimes you need the support of a supercool secretary. Do you have the courage to imagine your ideal situation free from anger and fear? And when you do imagine that ideal situation, will fear and anger get you there?

hall of
happiness

Decorating the Hall of Happiness takes no time at all.
You see, it's an empty room. For true happiness you don't
need anything at all. Happiness is a by-product of other things
like pleasure, relaxation, gratitude, meditation, peace. So here's
the fun part of the Hall of Happiness: it's not a room you can go
to or enter directly. You can't walk through a corridor, open a door,
and there you are in the Hall of Happiness; that's not how
happiness works. You can't approach happiness directly. You would
have to pass through the rooms of, e.g., Relaxation, Satisfaction,
or Fun first. You could then end up in the Hall of Happiness by
chance. You probably won't want to stay there for very long, though,
because apart from being extremely, purely happy, not a lot goes
on in there. It's very hard to measure the extent of happiness when
there's not much happening. Constant happiness gets boring.

Which rooms are connected to your Hall of Happiness?
Which personal chambers do you need to pass through to get here?
Is it a tea salon? Is it a dragon day care center? Is it a little study?
Is it a rose garden? Where on the floor plan of your Castle in the
Clouds will you place your Hall of Happiness?

# suite of shame

Shame is most often created by tension between your "true self" and your "ideal self"—between the real you and the person you would like to be.

You're ashamed when you trip on something and you would have preferred to be the one still standing. You're ashamed because you stumbled over your words when you would have preferred to be the one with the most eloquent and adequate answer. You're ashamed by your bad breath when you would have preferred to not stand out because of the odor of your mouth but rather because of other qualities you possess.

You're ashamed when you don't live up to your own expectations and those of your social environment.

That's why you could design a double room, a room en suite: one for your true self with the adjoining room for your ideal self. Then the two of them can help you have a clear understanding of where you are at and where you should be.

That way it can become a choice to be ashamed, and it won't force itself on you sneakily.

Shame mainly serves the community. If we approve of the same virtues and disapprove of the same vices, we become a unit—a group, a herd, a clan. And we need our group to survive. Maybe shame is a rudimentary social conscience, an emergency conscience just like a kangaroo baby that stays in the pouch, until it's developed enough itself. Shame internalizes itself until it becomes a full conscience making shame obsolete—if all goes well.

Shame is always about things that appear futile. Your conscience, who's pretty cool, will make sure you don't do anything too weird. You don't not kill someone because others might think that's lame but because deep down inside you know and can feel that it's something you don't want to do. By the same token, it's a lot more virtuous to end a relationship in a charming way because it feels right, not because you don't want his or her friends to speak badly about you. Or you know it feels good to take the bottles to the recycling center and not just because you're afraid of what the neighbors will think when they hear the glass tinkling in your garbage bags. Shame is about all those things another person could have an opinion about; conscience is about what is felt and known deeply within. Go conscience! Boo shame!

You could make a double room, with a connecting door, in your Castle in the Clouds to get a clear picture of your true self and the self you would like to be. The room on the left is for your true self. The room on the right is for a lifelike hologram that represents your ideal self, a projection of who you want to be or who you think you should be. (This projection could even change from event to event—with your in-laws you may want to be a different ideal self than at work or at a crazy party.)

Shame (the fear of not being good enough) drives you toward your beautiful, ideal, omnipotent projection. Every time you go through the sliding door to the room on the right, you have to pay a toll. The price for not being yourself is high. Every time you have the courage to be imperfect and you return to yourself in the room on the left, you make money, you gain value. That's what it's all about: having the courage to be imperfect. (Imperfect is, after all, based on certain social expectations. Flowers and plants are never imperfect. If they are not the same, they are simply a different species. The fewer there are of one type, the more exotic they are.)

Every time you are ashamed and would prefer to be your ideal self, you move to the room on the right. To open the sliding door, you need one of those credit card–type hotel keys. As soon as you slide it through the lock, it makes a withdrawal from your personal account.

For most people this means that they have accumulated a huge debt by the time they reach the age of twenty. They have spent more time in the room on the right than in the room on the left. They have probably adjusted themselves to others or situations more than choosing to stick to who they are. And that's perfectly normal. You could see it as a student loan. The time was needed to develop your own identity.

Kids learn almost naturally to adjust to their national culture. "This is how we do things." They learn to adjust to a family culture. "This is important to us." And growing up they learn to adjust (often of their own choice) to subcultures like peer groups, fraternities, sororities, clubs, study groups, work, etc. "This is who we are." "This makes us us."

You have followed all sorts of rules, regulations, and rituals more or less successfully. The payoff could be a rich social life. The downside could be that you have lived a projected life and created a conviction that nobody can love you for who you really are.

After the age of twenty is a good time to take stock, to pay off your debts, and to claim yourself back. You know what it's like to be accepted. You did it. You know what it's like not to be accepted, no matter how hard you've tried. You've had a pretty intensive training in trying to be perfect and to satisfy the world around you. How much did that cost you?

How much of your unique quirks and values have you had to submit to be a part of your world, your family, and your surroundings?

It would be interesting to print out every transaction: every move from shame to your ideal (costs), every move from courage to yourself (gain), and the total sum. Could you imagine what it would look like? What are the periods in your life when you saved or even enriched your personal account and on what periods or occasions did you make withdrawals from your personal account?

To get an idea of the grand total, you could look at the things you are ashamed of and your expectations about yourself. Are you living up to your own standards? Or do you have the (false) idea that you have to be something else to be loved (this could be a false idea, or you could be right, in which case you might want to consider changing social groups). Let's see how hard the next thought is for you.

### A SMALL EXERCISE IN IMPERFECTION

Here are three medallions you can earn by showing courage—the courage to accept your imperfections.

Imagine pinning them on your own chest. Two of these medallions are pretty general. The third is unique for you. It's for something you are ashamed about, something you are willing to face and therefore accept as an imperfection. What would it say on the third medallion?

Give yourself medallions for the courage of being imperfect.
Which "mistake" will you no longer consider a mistake or
shortcoming so you can stop being ashamed about it?

## DESIGN YOUR OWN IDEAL SELF

The hologram of your ideal self has designed itself over the years. From childhood you have thought about the expectations you had to meet. That's what your ideal self has based itself on with regular new additions. What the teacher would think of you, and the soccer coach, and your friends, colleagues, neighbors, the butcher, the barman, and the bus driver—it's all in there. That's how this ideal picture formed itself. Your ideal self should serve you instead of the other way around. Maybe the time has come to consciously make your own design the way you want it. That way you don't have to be ashamed of not being perfect (that is, if you are friendly to yourself while assembling) and you will be a bit closer to your true self, saving you from paying the price for alienation.

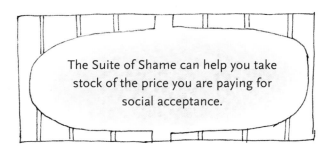

The Suite of Shame can help you take stock of the price you are paying for social acceptance.

Design the perfect picture of yourself

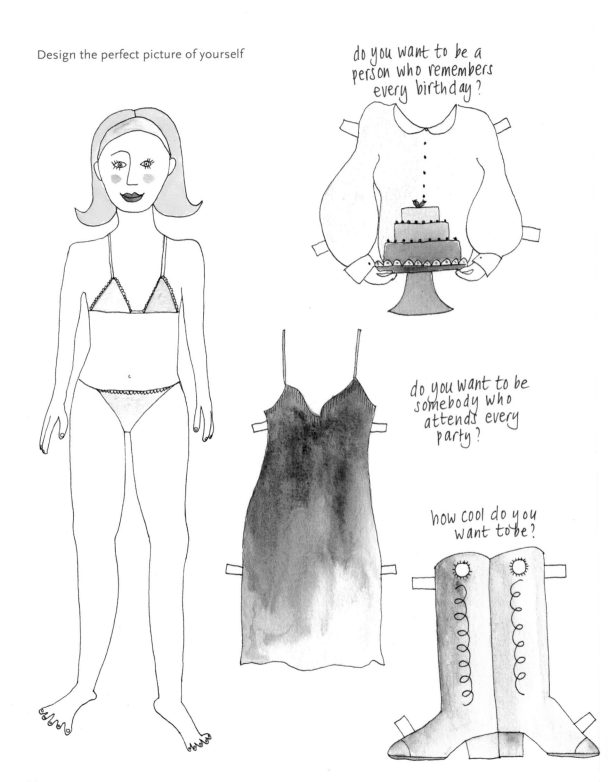

do you want to be a person who remembers every birthday?

do you want to be somebody who attends every party?

how cool do you want to be?

do you want to be someone who never burps?

how sexy do you want to be?

do you want to be somebody who remains true to him/herself at all times?

do you want to be a great cook?

do you want to be somebody who doesn't care too much about what others think?

# playroom

You feel tiny, yet completely safe in the Playroom.
You don't understand everything just yet, so you can look
around with wonder and amazement, you don't have any
responsibilities. It's that safe feeling you can have when
you're in the backseat of a car, driving through the night,
catching shreds of the conversation held up front.
Just enough to give you a sense of security,
but not enough to know what the
conversation is about.

You feel like a child on a long summer evening. The grown-ups are involved with each other, they are having fun, so there's nothing for you to worry about. You are doing your own thing. Everything is new for you. Everything is possible. You view the world through curious eyes. Everything is interesting, and you like everybody until they are unkind. You have all the time in the world, and everything is fun. You are a child the way children should be.

It feels like every breath gives you too much oxygen. You're excited. Your eyes twinkle. All your senses are switched on. You lick the pearls of condensation on the outside of a soda can. You listen to the creaking of the seat. You stroke the little dent between your nose and mouth with the back end of a spoon because it feels chilly and smooth. You smell your sheets until you are numb with the lovely scent of sleep. You pick at a small hole in a tree trunk with your finger and watch it grow bigger. That's how you feel.

You can still make your childhood dreams come true. Decorate a room in the way you would have loved it as a child.

What type of bed do you want? A bunk bed? A bed big enough to sleep eight? A sleeping alcove? A bed in the shape of a racing car? A hammock full of cuddly toys? Do you want a desk? Would you like a real little kitchen in your bedroom? Would you like a racetrack big enough for you to sit on that cruises through the shower too? Or would you prefer a tree house to a bedroom?

What toys would you give yourself? Give yourself three presents that would have made you ecstatically happy. Hide the three presents under your ideal bed as a surprise. Imagine waking up and looking under the bed. How would that make you feel? Since you're giving away presents, what gift would make you happy today? Is there a difference?

While you're in this ideal playroom, think of how you would like to be treated. What is it people should know to understand you? What are the rules of your playroom? What rules does everybody need to follow? Which laws have been followed and which have been broken? Which childhood dreams would you still want to come true? Which dream is finally going to be taken seriously and which dream should be let go of at last?

By whom do you want to be tucked in? Do you want to do it yourself? How would you do that? What story would you tell yourself? What's your favorite pillow, how does it smell, what does the bed linen look like, how tight do you want the sheets tucked in? Imagine putting you as a six-year-old to bed, stroking your own head softly, and how the six-year-old you slowly and happily drifts off to sleep. What would you say? What would be the last thing you would want to hear before falling asleep?

When you go to bed tonight, your bed in this reality, do you think you could tuck yourself in with a few comforting words instead of repeating a list of chores and must-dos, the length of which, the more you think about it and the later it gets, makes you more and more convinced you will never be able to complete it. What if you want to be nice to yourself, what would be the last words you would say to yourself before drifting off to sleep?

## THE BUNK BED

Imagine a bunk bed of seven layers. The middle one is for you. Underneath you are three people who give you a safe base; above you are three people who exhilarate you.

With which people can you feel like a child? Which people occupy the other beds?

Bed 1 is for someone you have known for a long time, someone who guards your past.

Bed 2 is for someone who makes you feel safe and careless.

Bed 3 is for someone whom you like to be touched by.

Bed 4 is for you, nice and snug in the middle.

Bed 5 is for someone you can have endless and senseless conversations and laughter with long after the others have fallen asleep.

Bed 6 is for someone you always have adventures with.

Bed 7 is for someone who always brings out the best in you.

It could make you feel sad if you don't know any people for your bunk bed. Rephrase the question. Who would you like to have had a past with? Who would you like to be careless with? By whom would you like to be touched? Who would you like to have endless laughter and conversations with? Who would you like to bring out the best in you? Who would you like to experience exciting adventures with?

## CHOOSE YOUR PARENTS

Now that you are in the process of creating a child's dream come true, you might as well pick your own parents too. You have a choice between safe and exciting. Why not both? You get to wish anything you want in your Castle in the Clouds, don't you? You may wish anything you want without pushing others into your wish. Because nobody is perfect, neither are your castle parents, and they seem very much like normal people. You do get to pick them though. Who will you choose? Are they like your own parents? Are they like the parent you are or think you will be? Pick them on appearance first, then by preferred character.

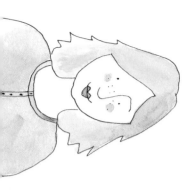

## MAMA A

The cuddliest mother made of softness, she reads to you and cooches, kneads and fuddles, and thinks you are a star. She makes the softest beds when you are feeling sick. She chases the monsters from underneath the bed too. She sews patches on your favorite jeans every time. She always finds you your favorite cuddly toy just before you go to sleep. She holds you when you're scared. She holds you when you're happy. She holds you when you have a tummy ache. She just doesn't ever want to let go of you.

Pick your own parents on looks first, then pick the character you prefer.

## MAMA B

A professional mother, she can do anything, and it seems she has a degree in motherhood. She runs the household like a military operation. Everything goes smoothly. She knows how to turn a pumpkin into a lantern, how to turn a toilet roll into a treasure, how to make funny faces out of broccoli. Every birthday party is celebrated at home, and she knows tons of entertaining games so all your friends always enjoy your parties the best. You live in a small, safe newly built neighborhood with lots of friends in the area. You're always allowed to bring friends home, and it doesn't matter how many—she'll raise those too. She has clean pairs of pants ready for when you or anybody else has fallen into a puddle. She's always on time for school plays, group pictures, handing in used batteries, newspapers, whatever. However there's little time left for conversation. When you come to her with a problem, she offers a funny solution, made of papier-mâché or something equally handy made out of an old egg carton.

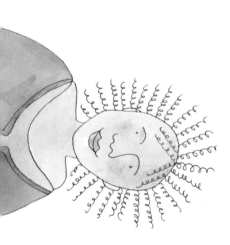

## MAMA C

She regards you almost as an equal. She gives you a lot of responsibilities, which builds your self-esteem. At an early age she takes you out for dinner and shows you the world. You always get to participate in conversations, and she always listens to your opinion. She doesn't treat you like a child, but has high expectations. Things have to be done her way. She has very little patience for balloons that burst, dirty pants, or the alligators hiding under the bed. She will help you with an essay for school—as long as you pick an adult topic. If the subject is guinea pigs, you're on your own.

### MAMA D

She's the career mother. From an early age there are babysitters and nannies. A whole week can go by without seeing her, because you are in bed by the time she gets home. She can't make it to school plays, and she was even late that one time she was supposed to pick you up from school. But when she is there, it is fun! Exciting and fun stuff happens. You go for lunch in a fancy restaurant. You go swimming with dolphins, and she laughs as if you're friends. You get to learn how to drive from her lap. The two of you do an impression of that prissy shop assistant and fall over with laughter. It's always fun ... that is, when she's around.

Pick your father too. Daddy A doesn't have to go with Mama A, you can make any combination. Do remember, however, that if this were real, some combinations would not guarantee the most harmonious atmosphere at home.

### DADDY A

The quiet home dad, he is back before dinner every night. He lives by the rules and expects the same from you. He makes you clean up your own room. He makes you clean your ears. He teaches you how to fix your broken bicycle. He takes time out to offer you quality time every day between 5:30 and 6:00 to do homework or to work on a project until it's done and you can start a new one. You get a goodnight kiss after dinner, and that makes the rest of the night free for himself.

### DADDY B

He's the career dad. You can be very proud of him because he makes tons of money and always gives you the very best and the most beautiful. On weekends he cheers you on at sports because your father loves to win. He will do his utmost to give you the best chances in life. He does see everything as a game—or a competition. For that matter he hates to see you lose, and he will be very disappointed in you when you haven't given something your best shot.

## DADDY C

This is the funny cuddly dad. The house is one big party place when you are together. Your room can look like a pirate ship for months. You have dinner on the roof. You get to sleep in your regular clothes, and if you want to go to school in your pjs, that's okay. He never gets angry (he will be in a lot of fights with most mothers though), and he's your best friend. Some things do tend to go wrong. He could take you to school only to find it empty—it turns out to be Saturday. There's moldy bread in your lunchbox. Or you might get home to find the door locked. Or you get to your swimming lessons with your ballet outfit in your swim bag. Be sure he'll find a funny solution.

## DADDY D

The intellectual dad, he's hardly ever there for you unless you have a problem or a major philosophical question. But then he will shove everything from his desk and talk to you long into the night. He is a bit scattered, and for years he can't seem to remember the name of your best friend. Sometimes he seems to look at you as if he's seen you somewhere before.

A Playroom in your Castle can be designed—to start with—to put something right from the past, where needed. Then you can look at your childhood dreams: For which ones has the time come to let go? Which ones are outdated? Which ones need to come true at last?

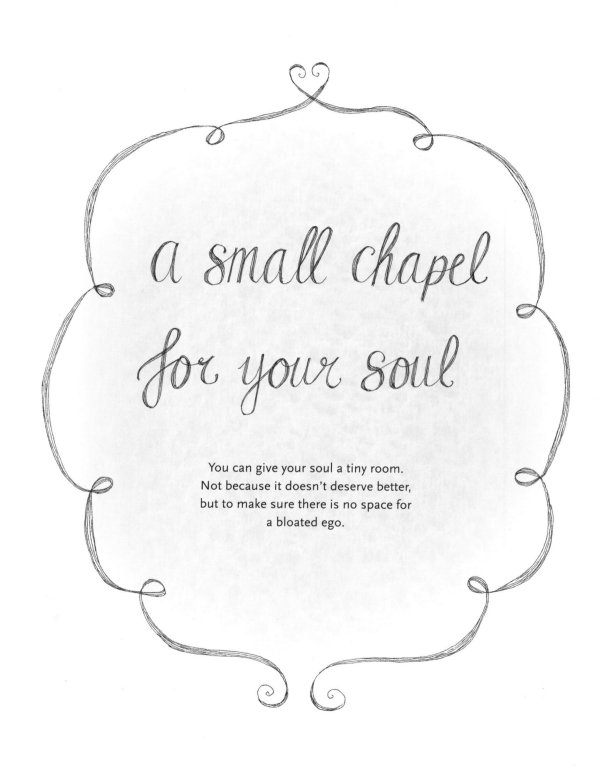

# a small chapel for your soul

You can give your soul a tiny room.
Not because it doesn't deserve better,
but to make sure there is no space for
a bloated ego.

Your soul speaks when you laugh out loud, when you tumble through the grass, when you love without holding back, when you forget about time, when you are radiant, when you enjoy, when you glow, when your eyes twinkle, when you cry a river, when you feel the wind in your hair.

Your ego rears up when you are irritated, frustrated, petty, mean, pissed off, when the coffee tastes bad, when your clothes tear, when the bus is late, when you are the only person acting normal and your lover is whining.

So, reserve a tiny, beautiful golden Chapel for Your Soul—and only for your soul. To go in, you will have to make yourself less important and deflate all the air from your ego. You must be completely bare without the padding of your bloated ego, which causes limited movement and means nothing or nobody can really touch you. Not being able to touch or be touched by anyone gives your soul a hopelessly misunderstood and lonely feeling.

Your ego is a self-inflating survival mechanism born out of the fear of falling short. It uses the same techniques as old-fashioned advertising: first, they scare you by telling you about the bacteria on your kitchen counter and then they sell you a hygienic spray. Ego scares you into thinking there is not enough love for you, too little respect, not enough recognition. Then it shows you techniques to win this love, respect, and recognition. Your ego kicks in when you try to control the free gifts you came with at birth or when you try to find these outside yourself.

That deep feeling of satisfaction and that huge sense of bliss you are seeking are within yourself. They can overwhelm you sometimes when you're having the best of fun, when you are totally lost in a physical challenge or working on something with incredibly focused concentration. That leaves no room for your ego. Well, that is, if it's ego-free fun, concentration, and attention. You can retreat into the Small Chapel for Your Soul to distinguish the difference.

## INTRINSIC VALUES

Your soul is ensured of a few intrinsic values like freedom, the sense of purpose,, the right to exist, trust, love and the connection with that which is larger and smaller all around you.

If you feel deep inside yourself at just the right moment, you know this is true; you can sense the freedom to be all that you are. If you are reading this at a time when you can't feel or believe this, don't resist it, just have the desire to believe it. "I wish I could truly believe that I am allowed to be all that I am, I feel full of love and trust that all is well as it is." That will do for now. If you ask yourself this question at the right moment, there are no doubts about your right to exist, it is no effort, just be. That's when you know it is true.

It's just like those times when you can feel with every fiber in your body that you are part of something much larger—not more important than anybody else

nor less important. Pity that this feeling isn't constant. These are the good moments. We often look outside of ourselves to be able to hold on to these values. That's when the problems start.

## A LITTLE EDGE OF EGO

The first step outside of your self (in other words, the soul) can feel quite nice. It makes you fun and funny —and that little edge of ego gives you an identity.

If you wanted to be only soul, you would be perfectly happy and satisfied with everything, but you would become a little otherworldly: an autistic-like Zen monk who smiles sweetly at a leaf that separates itself from the tree and floats down harmoniously, carried by that breath of air that unites us all. Good. Nice. But not very realistic unless we reinvent the entire world. That would be fantastic, but that's an entirely different book. This one is all about you. Nice!

You could make the door a little bigger in the design for the Chapel for Your Soul so that tiny little edge of ego fits through it too. But it is best to stick to the program and keep it solely for the soul, for you in its purest form. There's plenty of space for your ego in all the other rooms of your Castle in the Clouds; this room illustrates the slippery slope away from yourself, how easy it is for this to happen. The solution is not to search further but to let go of more. Letting go of false ego-driven ideas allows you to fit through the small door again, and you can then use your chapel as the perfect meditation room.

## VALUE-CONSTRUCTS

There's irritation and frustration on the outer edges of ego. You can't go much further. You have given the utmost of yourself, yet you feel far from satisfied, perfect, or happy. You are at your most ugly at the outer edge of ego: agitated, falling short, failing, narrow-minded, dissatisfied, incompetent, and very angry. How much more can you give? You're exhausted. (This happens when you focus on what's

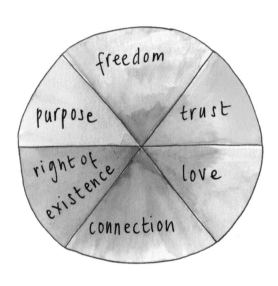

your soul

on the outside when you should be looking in. You're approaching it from the wrong angle!)

The places where it itches on the outside show you in which direction to look for a solution on the inside.
A value-construct is a concept of great importance to you. These are qualities that the ego uses to give itself worth and to inflate itself. If time is your value-construct, you measure events by how much time each one saves or costs you. If control is your value-construct, you settle up situations with the amount of control you will gain or lose. The same goes for value-constructs like respect, confirmation, acknowledgment, and impulse (how much distraction does it offer me?).

Which value-constructs do you recognize within yourself? One way to find out is to think of the things that irritate or frustrate you easily: think for example about a glass of milk spilled at breakfast—does it make you mad because it takes time to clean up? Does it annoy you because it feels like a lack of respect—no one is paying attention. Do you take on a soothing role because you want to make it easy for the guilty party? Is it because you don't want to break the connection? Does it annoy you that you did your best to lay a beautiful table and things happen that are out of your control?

## MODEL
Here's a model of a soul and ego so you can see what moving away from yourself does to you. To learn about yourself, you could observe from within to know what's important to you or by looking at your obsessions from the outside. That's not all though. Your soul and ego deserve a model of their own. You will have to come up with that one yourself. You could use this model as a guideline, erasing and replacing things with how they work for you.

## LOOKING FOR FREEDOM OUTSIDE YOURSELF
To own the feeling of ultimate freedom, autonomy, and authenticity, you may look outside yourself. The first innocent step out of yourself is the wish for self-development. That makes you fun.

The light, quick step outside yourself, the seemingly easy fix, is where you think you can only be free when you have money and can be autonomous. Money enables you to be who you are and do what you want to do, and everybody leaves you in peace. There's nothing wrong with money, but to make such huge amounts of it in order to gain freedom just means you are going to be incredibly busy. It will cost you a lot of time and energy. "Time" becomes your most valuable asset of worth. A value-construct is a concept of a trait that's important to you. If time is your value-construct, you will measure experiences by how much time it will cost or bring you. Your ego gets annoyed when the cars in front of you move too slowly, when the kids are finally dressed and then have to go to the bathroom. It puts you in a position directly opposite to freedom—that freedom you were trying to possess.

Retreat into the Small Chapel for Your Soul, rid yourself of all your set ideas about freedom, your expectations about your own identity, at the front door, and try to get back in touch with the deep sense of freedom that is a part of who you are.

## LOOKING FOR PURPOSE OUTSIDE YOURSELF
On a good day you can feel that everything you do is useful. On a bad day, ah well, you know.... To get a sense of purpose (something you already have deep within your being), you could look for it outside yourself. It starts innocently with an interest in your surroundings, but with it changing into curiosity comes an ability to further change into greediness, an insatiable greediness for new impulses, looking for the one that will stick.

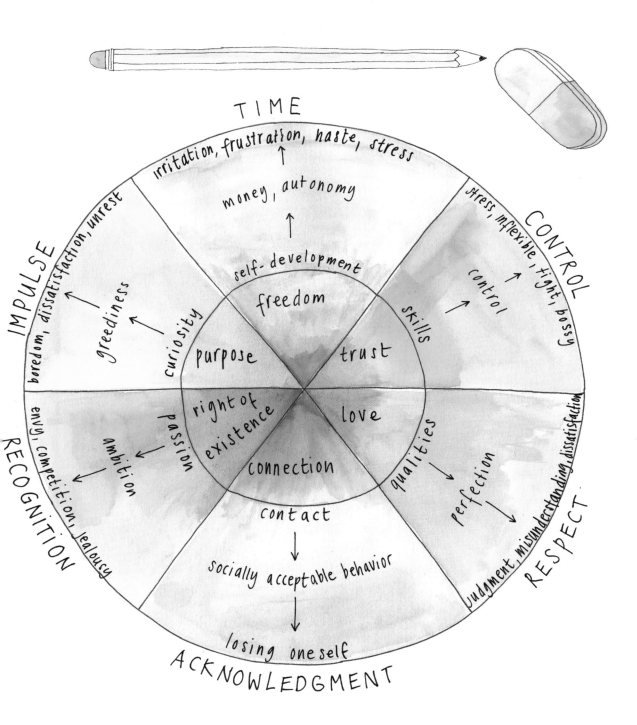

TIME

irritation, frustration, haste, stress

money, autonomy

CONTROL

stress, inflexible, tight, bossy

self-development

freedom

control

skills

IMPULSE

boredom, dissatisfaction, unrest

greediness

curiosity

purpose

trust

RECOGNITION

envy, competition, jealousy

ambition

passion

right of existence

love

judgment, misunderstanding, dissatisfaction

qualities

connection

perfection

RESPECT

contact

socially acceptable behavior

losing oneself

ACKNOWLEDGMENT

your bloated ego

Your ego gets an unstoppable hunger for experiences and emotions hoping to find the one thing that will release you from the constant desire for new and more. How often do you think: "If I have that, I won't need anything else, it will be done."

The euphoria of being complete is bizarrely short-lived because in essence it hasn't added anything to you. So boredom and dissatisfaction will ruthlessly move in. And wasn't the idea to feel a sense of purpose, to nurture it, keep it safe, and own it?

Could you go back to the Small Chapel for Your Soul and try to feel the core of your existence? It probably turns out to be something very precious, rather than huge and overwhelming, but it offers complete satisfaction if you can accept and value it. It's nothing more than that, but certainly nothing less. So instead of looking outside yourself, you can find it within in true intimacy.

## LOOKING FOR THE RIGHT TO EXIST OUTSIDE YOURSELF

A similar motion can be seen in looking for the feeling of the right to exist outside yourself; you think you have to be better than someone else to earn that right. The first fun step outside of your soul is passion. That easily shifts into ambition. You become competitive. When you try that hard, you want recognition. Your ego will then forcibly look for recognition because once is not enough. You want more recognition—and more than somebody else gets. Recognition cannot be commanded, you can't grant it to yourself and accept it.

If you often catch yourself feeling jealous (of those who compare up), contemptuous (of those who compare down), pushy, exerting willpower, then recognition could be your value-construct. It might help to retreat into the Small Chapel for Your Soul and allow yourself to meditate on the thought that you don't have to do anything for the right to be/exist.

## LOOKING FOR TRUST OUTSIDE YOURSELF

It feels a little naive and silly to have total trust. It's the tourist wandering around with that look of amazement and innocence who gets robbed. You and I know better. With a slightly skeptical outlook on life, we will be safe. We are attentive and alert to our surroundings. This is about the little trust. In order to navigate life outside yourself, you must qualify in skills. You think you have to be able to do things, make things tangible, to bring order, to be able to manage, to name it, compiled as skills. Your ego wants control, thinks it has control, or thinks it needs control. If you often feel anxiety, stress, tightness, or frustration, it could be that control is your value-construct, because control is never 100 percent feasible and therefore always frustrating. Here you are, trying to possess/own the little trust when it is in fact about the big trust—trust that you can handle any reality at the precise moment it comes up. Believe that all will be well, and until that time, let go of your fears. It's very scary, but not as scary as wanting to control everything.

Retreat into the Small Chapel for Your Soul and meditate or reflect or simply desire a deep sense of trust that not only all will work out in the end, but all is well as it is. It could help you. If you can imagine how universal and all-encompassing trust feels, you are actually already there.

## LOOKING FOR UNCONDITIONAL LOVE OUTSIDE —AND FINDING IT WITHIN YOURSELF

You may think you can guarantee unconditional love outside yourself by being perfect. The first innocent step is striving for qualities. ("I'll make sure I'm nice, thoughtful, faithful"—those kinds of things.) But however innocent, you can only recognize virtues and qualities by comparing yourself to others. In a comparison you most likely want to be the better one. The need to be perfect rears up. Everybody will have to love you when you're perfect.

When you manage to be reasonably perfect (according to your own standards), you might find you have spent quite a lot of time before you realize that doing everything right and expecting the same from those around you do not equal love. Perfection has nothing to do with love.

When you don't do so well at being perfect (according to your own standards), you realize sooner that you are not receiving enough love. You could blame that on the (self-conjured) idea that you are not sufficient or your surroundings are not sufficient or a happy marriage of the two.

In both cases you are very busy judging and comparing. Am I receiving enough, am I doing well, is somebody else doing better? Both cost a lot of effort (proving to yourself and others that you and yours are doing well and proving to yourself and others that you and yours are not doing well). In both cases the ego will appoint an unnatural importance to respect. If you don't get the love you think you deserve, you should at least be respected. Respect for the effort you are putting in, respect for your needs, respect for where you came from, respect for your strife. Love is just granted, but we think we can control respect. It's okay to say: "I demand respect" at the family dinner table, with friends, or even in a meeting. Nobody would say; "I demand love" (can you imagine?!).

Do you think you can go to the Small Chapel for Your Soul and let go of the idea of perfection in order to create space for true love? You can't force love or command it, but you can learn to recognize it for what it is. There are so many more varied ways to it than pink postcards and steamy movie kisses. It's all around you, it's all in you. It is you.

## LOOKING FOR A CONNECTION OUTSIDE YOURSELF

On bad days, you can doubt the deep universal union your soul came with for free (because it's part of a larger whole) at birth. The urge to hold on to the sense of connection seduces your ego to present itself in a very sociable way and to comply with those things you think are expected from you. You make contact by stepping outside yourself toward others. On a small scale it's nice, wanting to make contact; sometimes you need to be touched, seen, or heard by another person in order to feel that you exist. But how long does it take for your ego to expect something in return?

Ego wants confirmation and will start to display socially desirable behavior. Look how good I am at this little trick (and people who tend to pick this strategy are usually pretty good at making friends). You feel good as long as things go well; you can handle the world because you think you can manipulate reality. Apart from the fact that this is extremely tiring, it often leads to losing complete sight of (or, better said, complete heart in) yourself.

The sense of true connection with everything and everybody around you is a decision of the heart—of your heart—and not a choice made by the people, things, and animals you want to connect with. Funnily enough, they have very little to do with it. That's why you can connect perfectly, all alone, in meditation, in the Small Chapel for Your Soul. The connection between you and everything in the universe down to the tiniest baby hedgehog is constantly there. It's just soft, polite, discreet.

## THE ANTIDOTE FOR A BLOATED EGO

It's an old miracle cure: pure undivided attention.
It's hard not to love something that has your complete attention. You could possibly turn it around: when you don't love something or someone, you don't give it enough attention. Your ego deflates like a soufflé as soon as you are enjoying yourself, when your full consciousness is engrossed in something, when you do the things you love, or when you are in the company of people you love.

The ego is badly equipped to deal with undivided attention (for something other than itself) in the same way a vampire can't handle garlic.

### EGOLESSNESS

Can you imagine how you would feel without any ego? If all you are is trust, unity, and love in ultimate freedom? How would you feel as you touch everybody and are connected to all, because that airbag around you has disappeared? How much careless fun could you have? Who would you be? How would you react to some of the things that tend to frustrate and irritate you now?

### DECORATING THE SMALL CHAPEL

You have a beautiful little door to start with. What do you need for meditation? A yoga bench, a cushion, a straight chair? An altar, incense, candles, music? Are the walls made of gold, felt, or wool? Would you like a little dome for looking at the stars? Do you like pillars? Do you want a little room high up in a tower with four windows facing the four winds? Or would you prefer the ground floor in direct contact with the earth? What color is the Small Chapel for Your Soul? What flower is in a little vase? What does your soul need (oxygen, light, music, space, harmony, comfort)?

### THE FALSE IDEA BOX

You must get rid of the false ideas of the ego in order to feed your soul. There's a garbage can in front of the door to your Chapel. You can dump everything in the bin before you go in—every time. You don't have to succeed in getting rid of all these ideas in one go. Look at it as an exercise. Unload little by little every time.

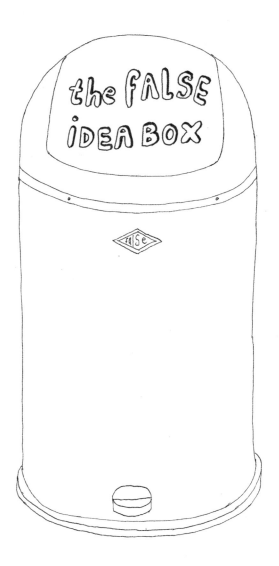

## 1. THE RIGHT TO EXIST

To get closer to the sense of your right to exist, you must let go of the idea that you have to do anything or accomplish anything to have the right to be. It has been beautifully said: we are human beings, not human doings. You may have heard it more than once, but it's too true not to mention again.

## 2. CONNECTION

Let go of the idea that there is a difference between you and me.

## 3. LOVE

Let go of all the ideas you may have about love—what it should look like or how it should feel. And more: that it has to be answered or measurable, that it comes in shapes you can compare, that there might not be enough, that you do or don't deserve it, that you should receive as much as you give, how to recognize it, hold on to it, that you have to feel it, that you're not allowed to feel it.

## 4. TRUST

Let go of the idea that you have to be able to influence anything. Let go of your attachment to problems and drama. Let go of the thought that things will not work out unless you interfere.

## 5. FREEDOM

Let go of all expectations, frameworks, and results.

## 6. PURPOSE

Let go of the idea that life should mean anything, or it's worthless.

> You can design a Small Chapel for Your Soul in your Castle in the Clouds in order to gain awareness of the difference between your soul and your ego, in order to get closer to your true self.

# inner courtyard

Imagine that there is a place where you feel completely safe.
In the olden days, the Inner Courtyard of a castle was a secure
place, enclosed by high, thick walls with holes to shoot from
and patrolling guards on watch. Imagine your Inner Courtyard
in your Castle in the Clouds as a space where you can play,
enjoy, and be carelessly free. You're safe and thus free from
criticism (including your own!), safe from the news of the
world, safe from those people who put pressure on you.

What do you need to feel completely safe?
What do you need to be protected from?

Who could you
be if you were totally
free from fear?

What does your Inner Courtyard look like
and what are you doing there?

Who can't cross that wall ever,
not even to take a peek?
Who do you need to keep an eye on?
Who'll never cross your boundaries?

## THE GUARD DOGS

You can have several guard dogs in your Inner Courtyard. They'll warn
you of situations that could make you feel unsafe, unless you react
differently. Which guard dog would be useful to you at the moment?

wesson   &   smith

## WESSON (SMITH'S BROTHER)

Wesson clenches his jaws and growls loudly when you are about to say more than you want to or should, when you are about to apologize or when you are about to defend yourself, or when you start talking gibberish to avoid a silence. He is in fact showing you what to do. Clench those jaws together. You don't have to explain to the shop owner why you are not buying what's on sale. You don't have to explain in a restaurant that you've been sick all day therefore did not finish what was on your plate. That doesn't make anybody happier. You don't have to tell anyone that you have to be at your child's recital at school—"I have an appointment" will do. You don't have to be the first to break the silence during negotiations.

## SMITH (WESSON'S BROTHER)

Smith starts barking like mad when you are about to make a promise to do something you don't have the time or energy for. You could take it on if you had an endless supply of energy, but you don't. He barks when you're in a situation already that is costing you too much energy or when you come into contact with a person who drains you of your energy. He barks to warn you to take action: say no, stop listening, end the conversation with a friendly smile. You have to take charge, that's the idea, but if you can't, stroke Smith's head and say: "I know, I've noticed, you're right, but this time it can't be done." Smith will calm down, but he keeps a sharp eye on you.

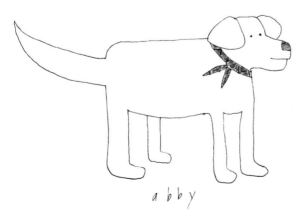

abby

## ABBY

Abby is a faithful Labrador who wags her tail happily and whacks you with it when you take things that are happening too seriously or when there is something that makes you feel aggrieved or angry or irritated. She helps to remind you that you can react in a different way: lighter. So wag your own tail too.

## REX

Rex bites your hand softly when you let someone walk all over you. He bares his very sharp little teeth and shows you how to do the same. It is time to set your boundaries, to take the space you need. Let them know these endless jokes are no longer appreciated, that you want to be heard, that it's okay to make more money, that you want to dance, that you want to be happy, that you want to laugh.

r e x

## WOLF

Wolf starts howling when you let your own thoughts scare you.

wolf

When you are feeling uncomfortable in any given situation, what dog would be the best one to guard you, for that specific issue? Naturally the refinement comes from you. When does Abby catch on, when does Rex? In the beginning you might have to train them when to bark and growl. This is a typical Smith moment: "Oh, it's perfectly fine that you have to leave earlier, I will take care of it." A typical Wesson situation: "Yeah right, I'm sorry . . ." and all that follows. Smith & Wesson operate together a lot by the way, they are from the same litter.

What other guard dogs do you think you might need?

An Inner Courtyard in your Castle in the Clouds can help you find your weaknesses. And you can learn how you can keep them safe with the right guard dogs.

# art studio

The Art Studio in your Castle in the Clouds is a place to
be creative. To be truly creative, for original thinking and
to surprise yourself, you can only allow the artist into your
Art Studio, never the gallery owner. The artist just wants
to create and will then decide what to call it later on.
The gallery owner can't wait to name it, think of a buyer,
and what to ask for it, often before it has even
been finished.

The gallery owner is not easily overenthusiastic or positive. She often says things like: "What is that? I have never seen anything like it before. Nobody is waiting for that. It will never sell." That's why she manages a gallery and did not become an artist herself. So in your head you only allow the artist into your Art Studio. The artist is focused on the process; the gallery manager is focused on results.

You don't let the artist do the administration, and you don't let the gallery manager touch the paintbrushes. When you split off the artist and gallery manager from each other like Siamese twins, you will be left with the pure original spirited practical energy of the artist. Practical, yes, because he (or she) wants to produce and make things.

To get the artist ball rolling again, you should just get started. It's best to let your hands begin, to get into that super feeling also known as flow, that feeling that comes over you when you lose yourself in what you're doing, oblivious of time. If you want to write, start writing. It doesn't matter what. Start putting down letters that make words that form sentences on paper. Don't stop, keep going. And pleasantly ask the gallery owner to go to her Gallery. You can be a little less friendly about it if she keeps showing up. You see, you have to keep writing, there is a moment when it flips and it actually turns into something—a letter, a story, an insight. The beginning is like a very heavy gearwheel that has to be set in motion by hand, but once it gets started, there's no stopping it. It's important to keep faith in the moment when it flips. It's important to trust the tipping point will come. There are often a few painful hurdles before you get to that point: "Where is this leading, it's never going to work, I quit, it's stupid, the world is stupid, I am stupid." Those hurdles are proof that the gallery manager is

art studio

## art studio

still around trying to sneak a peek. Give her a huge kick in the butt if you have to. Don't think, just write. Write nonsense, or so-called nonsentences. These nonsentences are necessary to get to the sentences that make sense.

You keep the possibilities open as long as you trust, keep the faith. And all of a sudden it just happens, you can't remember when and how: the writing just seems to come without effort. That is the magic of the artist. The Art Studio helps with this. You could call it inspiration, that trust that it will come, as long as you start, remain open, and do not stop writing, painting, crocheting, doing what you want to do.

It's the same with drawing. Start with your hands and a pencil on a piece of paper. Send the gallery manager on her way and keep going to the point where your efforts flip and unfold into something. This is still not the moment to label it as anything. Later, when you're at the Gallery with the gallery owner, you can look at what you've made and give it a name. Funnily enough, she is pretty creative and inventive with that. She has the ability to look at something that exists and see all its possibilities. She can see the opening line of a great song in a bad route description (At the dark end of the street . . .). A slightly burned dish can turn out to be a fantastic new recipe. A bad novel can be great therapy.

A bad idea can be the kick start to a brilliant world-conquering insight.

When it is hard for an artist to let go of a work—and it is sometimes—it is time to hand it over to the gallery owner. You can decide where you want to be at that stage of the process, in the Art Studio to make work or in the Gallery to assess the work and show it to the world.

When the creative process isn't flowing, it usually is not clear where the project is at that moment in time—in the Art Studio (in creation) or in the Gallery (in assessment). If it feels like the process is blocked, it means you're in between rooms. Pick where you are. Choose either of the two, both are fine, but don't mix the energy of the artist with the energy of the gallery owner. Together they block the creative process; by themselves they both can manifest an explosion of inventiveness.

The qualities of the artist:
1. He/she possesses an immeasurable energy that can be focused on one thing.
2. He/she is open to absolutely everything.

# gallery

The Gallery in your Castle in the Clouds is a place to show the work you have made, from the Art Studio, for example. Here your work is displayed in the best light, and you sell it with the best arguments. That's the perfect job to let the gallery manager handle.

*gallery*

To start out with, you thank the artist from the heart for the work, and then you push him/her out of the shop. Galleries make artists nervous, and a gallery manager can't make deals with the artist around. There comes a time when the artist has to distance himself from his work and all that was felt and thought in the process, however interesting.

The gallery manager looks at the work that's there at that moment. She looks at it realistically and has the gift to see all its possibilities. Maybe it isn't a film script but a beautiful short story instead. It might not be the perfect design for an apartment block, but it could be a great trash can—or the other way around.

*gallery*

There's never anything wrong with the work itself. It could be named wrong though. And then you could just change how you call it, name it, or label it. The work itself just is. And the gallery manager will use her sharp, inventive, and analytical thinking to come up with the suitable name to manifest the work in the world.

She possesses a kind of practical creativity. This is in contrast to the artist's purely abstract creative power. Practical creativity is looking at existing things, comparing them with each other, and discovering a new pattern. Pure creativity has nothing to do with anything that already exists; something entirely new unfolds.

If you can't manage to love, defend, or sell your work, it means the artist is still around. The shy artist might be dragging you into his or her insecurities. Send the artist to the Art Studio, letting him or her know that all will turn out for the best, but right now, in this part of the process you don't need the floaty, wishy-washy, everything-is-possible, all-is-magic mentality of the artist.

In order to sell your work (and this doesn't have to be for money, the trade-off could also be time from your family, more freedom from your employer, or your own permission to proceed), you must make an unequivocal decision: what is it, why is it good, what will it mean to people, and what does the artist in you want in return (money, time, space, permission)? That's what the gallery manager is good at. She will stand for your work 100 percent. She defends and praises it. She has the guts to advertise what you love without worrying if someone will buy it.

It may seem as if the artist and the gallery manager aren't friends, but that's not true. They are fine meeting in different rooms of your Castle in the Clouds. When they are working, however, they each have to be on their own territory, without the interference of the other. They have one of those beautiful, newfangled LAT relationship (living-apart-together). Keep it that way.

In case it has escaped your notice, you are the gallery manager. Try to imagine having her skills. You have the courage to believe in yourself. You are also the artist. Visualize yourself with unstoppable energy and have the guts to trust that inspiration will come as long as you keep going. So, you are the gallery manager, you are the artist, but most of all you are the one who can consciously switch between the two.

The qualities of the gallery owner are:
1. She/he can cast an inventive look at things that already exist.
2. She/he has the guts to make a decision and to defend that choice with great enthusiasm.

The Art Studio in your Castle in the Clouds can help you to be creative without boundaries. The Gallery can help you sell your creativity without shame.

# ballroom

Host an elaborate party, invite all
the personalities within you,
and celebrate who you are—completely.

One of the many parties you could host in your very own Ballroom is one in honor of yourself—where you are the radiant center of attention. But who are you exactly? You are made of many facets, idiosyncrasies, and voices. So invite them all. That way you get to know all the glorious aspects of you.

You could make a grand and royal gesture, even to the nastiest voices within. This time they will not come and interfere with your life, uninvited and unexpected, you are inviting them yourself. They can show themselves and be heard, but only on your terms.

And who might you be when all your identities are standing there sipping champagne in their best outfits? Naturally you are the hostess or host, the head honcho, the one in charge. You welcome them all one by one. You put personalities in the spotlight. You decide who gets the mic. You decide who is the guest of honor. You say when it's time to go. It's your bigger self who pulls the strings—the Real You.

To make sure you won't forget anybody, here's a checklist of every possible personality and voice that you could have and should therefore invite.

Who will think of themselves as your most important guests?
Who would you prefer not to have invited?
Who comes together, who makes themselves invisible?
Who are your most important guests?
Who would you like to name as your guests of honor?

The celebration of me,
myself, and I

## THE GUEST LIST

The dreamer
The spiritual one
The happy one
The proud one
The fearful one
The consumer
The egoist
The shy one
The ambitious one
The jealous one
The envious one
The manipulative one
The arrogant one
The bossy one
The codependent one
The lonely one
The autonomous one
The individualist
The adventurer
The critic
The diva
The radiant one

The sweet one
The cute one
The lighthearted one
The depressive one
The funny one
The irritating one
The meddling one
The gossip
The stubborn one
The fantasist
The realistic one
The sensuous one
The flirt
The romantic one
The sporty one
The uncomplicated one
The competitive one
The sentimental one
The dramatic one
The loving one
The intelligent one
The philosopher

The perfectionist
The slow one
The sharp one
The positive one
The inventive one
The negative one
The sigher
The caring one
The mother
The father
The child
The social one
The asocial one
The invisible one
The magical one
The pleaser
The creative one
The sorcerer
The voluptuous one
The charming one
The refined one
The sensitive one

## TIPS FOR A SUCCESSFUL PARTY

Start by welcoming everybody personally. When each comes in, you hold the identity's hand briefly and say: "I'm so glad you are here, was it easy for you to find me?" And imagine what their answers would be.

A fun party is always slightly unpredictable. That's why it's a good idea to keep certain people away from each other. Fear, Drama, and Pride like hanging out together, and the outcome of that party is pretty obvious.

Separate your friends from your acquaintances. Pride is an important voice, one you can't do without, but you don't need all the hangers-on Pride always brings along, like the Manipulator, the Egoist, the Asocial One, and the Competitor. Be a good host(ess) and introduce Pride to the Caring and the Invisible Ones. They are so used to taking a few steps back that a conversation between them and Pride would create a completely different dynamic.

## TABLE SEATING

Prior to the party is a small intimate dinner with your guests of honor, your own seven key figures. For most people these key figures are:

- Power (such fun if you place him next to Joy rather than Anger. If they manage to become friends, the development of power could be totally different.)

- Love (as long as her pals Drama, Sentiment, and Romance aren't around, she is free of shame)

- Joy (without mates like the Consumer and the Gossip who always want to be first in line. What does pure solitary Joy have to say to you?)

- Fear (without any of its acquaintances to make sure it can only speak purely for itself)

- Pride (without its nervous friend Fear. In the right context Pride will make sure you take good care of yourself, bring out the best in yourself and enjoy it. A noble personality as long as you keep him away from Fear and Egoism.)

- The Child (with all its vulnerability, but also its creative and magical sides. You might want to keep the Child away from the Realist and the Pessimist.)

- The Light (your higher self, the main tenant of your Castle in the Clouds, the Real You, your spiritual side, your connection to All—give it a name. Strike up a conversation, and you will see that he/she will always be there for you, you just might not listen enough. Ask for his/her opinion on some of the issues that are relevant in your life at this very moment.)

## OPENING LINES

You can hold this dinner at the table in your Castle in the Clouds or at home at your kitchen table, just make sure you will not be disturbed, because it could look a little strange to others. Seat yourself at the head of the table and look at the name tags for your seating arrangement. Here are a few opening lines you could use to start up a conversation. After you have asked the question, change seats. Take the seat of the one who is to answer you. Try and immerse yourself completely in his or her personality and answer the host(ess)/Real You in the name of your guest. You could do all of this in your head, but it has a far greater effect if you actually shift seats (but again, you might want to make sure no one is around).

To Power: "How are you?" (Okay, you could have come up with that one all by yourself, sorry.) "What's been keeping you busy lately?" "How can I make better use of you?" "What do you stand for?" "Is that truly what you want?"

To Love: "What do you need to feel totally free?" "Is there something you would like to tell me?" "Do I give you enough space?" "Would you like to be my main voice for a while?" "What do you think would happen if you were?"

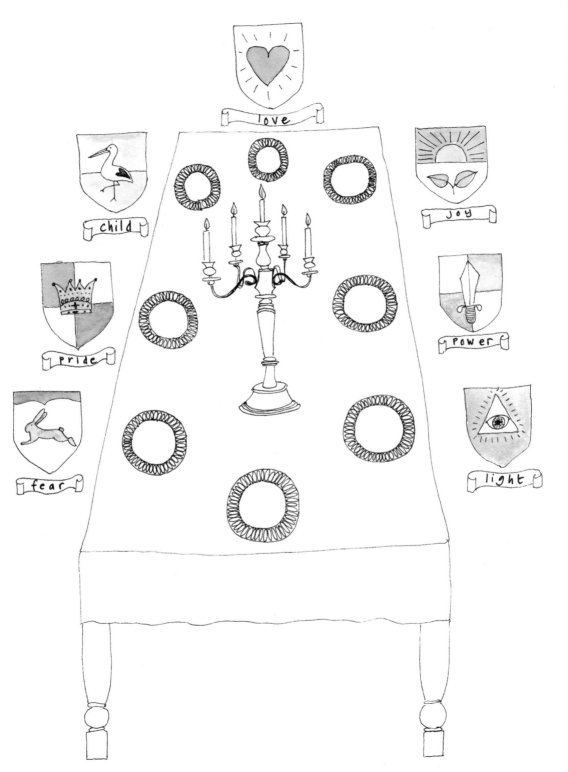

To Joy: "How can I be more aware of you?" "What are the things that hold you back?" "How can I make more time for you?"

To Fear: "So good to have you here, that means all of us can relax." (Fear is very sensitive about recognition.) "If I promise to really listen to you, do you think you will be able to relax a little bit too?" "Would you like a drink? A virgin mojito perhaps?"

To Pride: "Are you keeping busy?" "Do you enjoy being that busy?" "Even if you played a smaller part, you'd still be very important. If you insist on doing something, do you think you could be proud of all of these people here at the table rather than just being proud of yourself?" "As far as I'm concerned it would be perfectly acceptable if you took on a passive role and just observed to see what you would like to be proud of rather than actively aiming and hunting for pride, how would you like that?" "Would you take the Invisible One under your wing for a while, the one who always makes him/herself smaller?"

To the Child: "How do you feel about this?" "Whose lap would you like to crawl up on?" "What would you like to do right now more than anything?" "Are you happy?"

To the Light: "Do you know why I listen to you so rarely?" "It's sometimes hard for me to hear you because you are so humble. Please stick with me."

You can invite anyone you like to this dinner and even let "bad" qualities vent. Acknowledging a voice leads to control over it, so that you, the host or hostess, has the final say. If you deny the negative aspects of yourself, they will sabotage your party or hang around in other parts of your Castle in the Clouds. So, throw a party once in a while, get them drunk, and make sure they get the chance to be seen and heard. Listen to everybody and make it clear that all of them belong there. Thank them all for coming and embrace them all. All these voices make you who you are.

V.I.P.

What if you could only invite a limited number of people to your party. If you could invite only ten personalities, who would you ask? Who makes you? What if you could invite only six personalities?

And what if (yeah, you could see this one coming), you could invite only three personalities? An extremely exclusive party. Which three personalities are the most essential part of you? You may want to answer this question in a different way. Which three personalities would you like to give the most important voices? Is there a difference between who you are and who you want to be? Could you try to invite those personalities who can help you be the person you want to be and let their voices be heard for a while? Practice from within your Castle in the Clouds. Try to see things through the eyes of Joy or Love (or whomever you want) for a while and see if it touches reality.

Visualizing a feast for all the personalities within yourself can help you discover new aspects of yourself. And it's a strategy to figure out which guests deserve more or less attention from you from now on.

# your garden of wishes

You can plant wish seeds in the Garden of Wishes. And if you take good care of them and take them seriously, your wishes will come true. A wish seed is something you want badly, and at the same time, it is a promise to yourself that you will give some serious attention to this need. Attention is the most powerful fertilizer you can think of (in a positive and negative way as it happens). A wish takes the shape of a seed, because everything in the wish is potentially already here, just like in a seed.

## FORMULATING YOUR WISH

This is how you do it. You formulate your wish. You do that by starting with: "I wish for myself . . ."

Yes, wish seeds are always for yourself. You can only manifest your own wishes. The most important part of the magic formula is that all the words are positive. Like affirmations. So you say; "I wish complete faith for/in myself" rather than saying: "I wish myself no fear." The word fear works as a vise on your heart even if you mean "no fear." It's like screaming: "don't panic, don't panic!"—it makes a lot of people very uneasy. Nobody get's sad when somebody shouts: "no love, no love!" because all the heart can hear is the word love.

Feel the difference between these two sentences, in essence they say the same thing, but they carry a world of difference.

I am unhappy.

or

I want to be happy.

So.

You formulate a wish. You say this wish out loud and plant it in your Garden of Wishes. You have to water and nourish the wish seed every day; it needs feeding. You can do this by saying your wish out loud twenty times.

Pick a set time to do this. You have an abundance of freedom in your Castle in the Clouds, very few obligations, but feeding your wish is a priority.

## PERMISSION TO WISH

Giving yourself permission to have desires is the first step toward your wish coming true. This is the hardest step, in fact. Keep faith. Try to imagine the outcome of your wish. Go on, imagine.

What is keeping you from seeing it crystal clear before you? That probably has to do with courage or the lack of it rather than with the ability or inability of creating reality as you want it. This might be the scariest thing there is. This is the real dragon you have to slay to get to the well of abundance: the fear of not becoming who you want to be. The fear of failing could stop you from allowing the dream to continue. You can slay the dragon by looking it straight in the eye and thinking: "Despite the fact that you might think this is not going to work, it is what I want." And see the picture of your wish in your head.

Going into the discussion and making it about willpower: "I will succeed, you are all wrong" leaves you vulnerable because you have to waste energy defending your skills and your being right. No go. However, the wish itself is indisputable. The only possible answer every time is: "Whatever, possibly, but this is what I want." Stick to it and you will get stronger.

> ☉ Never give up on a wish ☉ because you doubt the outcome. Things usually go wrong at the beginning of the wish, not the ending; more wishes have been given up on than ☉ haven't come true. ☉

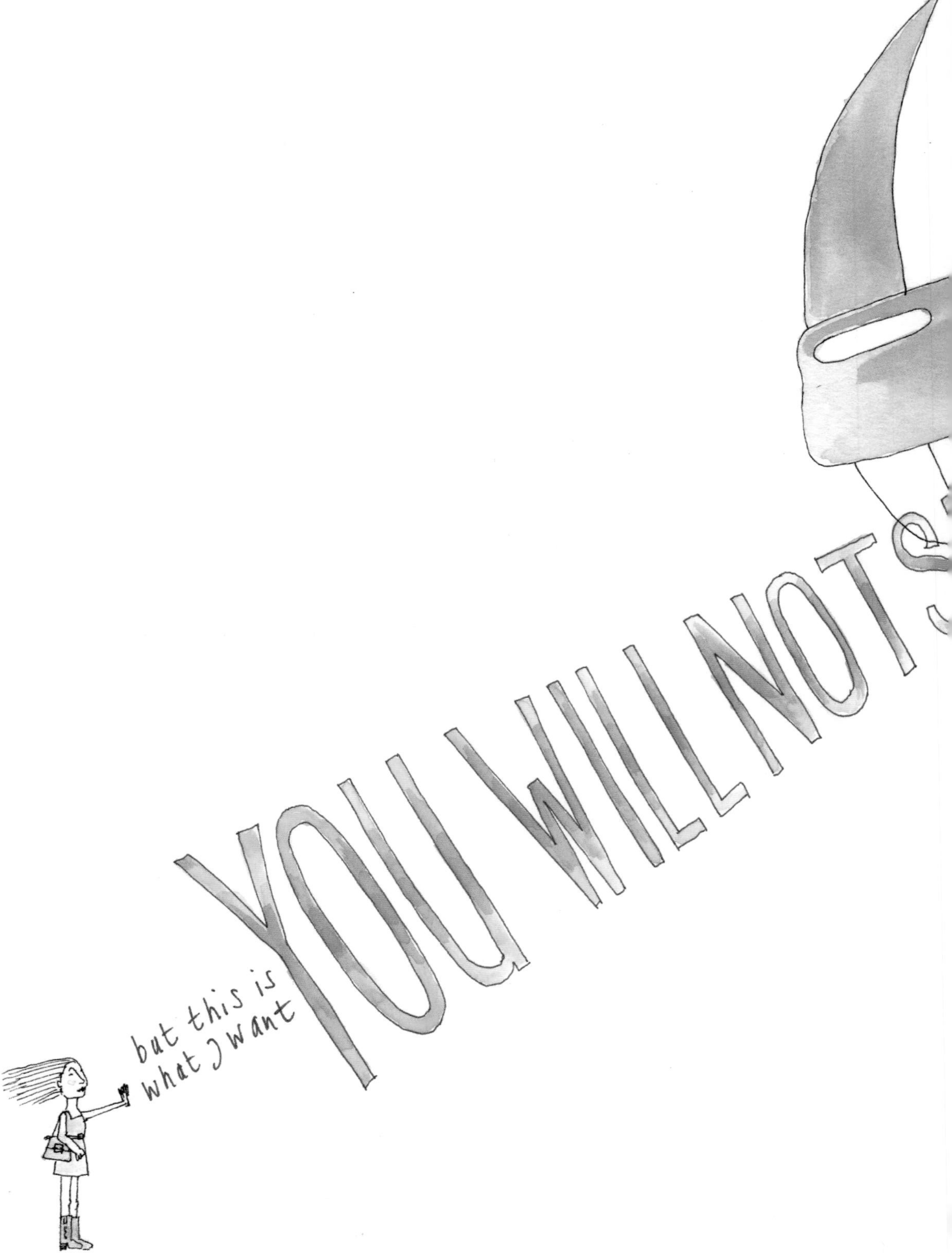
but this is what I want
YOU WILL NOT

## GRATTITUDE TREE

The best place to plant your wish seed is in the shadow of a Gratitude tree. This is a tree with leaves on it that you can use to write out the things that you are grateful for. Being grateful on command seems to throw you back in time—"Well, what do you say?" when you've just received a present. Gratitude is best experienced by enjoying something thoroughly and not so much by politely saying thank-you. A tree bears fruit as long as it's picked.

Before you plant your wish seed, stand still and remember the things you had fun with, that you enjoyed, yes, that you are grateful for. You could write these down daily to make you more aware of all the things, people, and events that make life so valuable. This will create fertile soil for new wishes. Abundance is the plural of gratitude.

The next thing you do is express your wish twenty times. Then you leave it up to the garden to make it come true. Give it at least forty days. Forty days are what a seed needs to sprout. Forty days are also the amount of time an act needs to become a habit.

In this reality you could write your wish on a tiny note and put it in a little flowerpot. Place the pot on your desk or on a windowsill and "water" it twenty times every day. Or you could use an empty jam jar, or in a little pouch around your neck, or you could write it on the bathroom tiles with soap. You can repeat the wish by stirring your soup twenty times.

It's too easy to say that all your wishes will always come true. When you wish for a million dollars before the next sunrise, it doesn't necessarily happen. Or to be able to walk when you are completely paralyzed. Or to get George Clooney to fall head over heels in love with you. That has nothing to do with the come-true factor of wishes; it's about the type of wish, because some of these wishes are physically impossible. The deeper needs can come true if you formulate the wish properly: "I wish to feel rich." "I wish to be at peace with my situation." "I wish for a partner that I will find equally as exciting as George Clooney."

a body radiating with good health

financial independence

the Love of my Life

prefab wishing seeds

*my wish ♡*

## WHAT IS YOUR WISH

Time to make some wishes. What is your wish? Is it worth saying your wish twenty times a day for the next forty days? Or is that price too high? (It's a total of 800 times.) If it isn't, then formulate your wish and make the following deal with yourself:

1. I will give my wish the attention it needs for the next forty days by repeating it twenty times each and every day.

2. I will trust that all will be well.

3. I am open to any way my wish might come true. In other words (and let this be clear), I will not force, push, or think about how my wish should come true.

Your Castle in the Clouds Garden of Wishes can help you admit to your desires. It can help you to become aware of the language you speak out loud and softly within. Do you express yourself in negatives or in possibilities? Do you bring about a wish-fulfilling prophecy in this way?

a deep connection with the universe

to stay close to MYSELF under all circumstances

A heart Overflowing with ABUNDANCE

SATISFACTION in everything I do

You could use one of the prefab wish seeds.

for the
dixie chicks

eet that
nat you
ant them
to do

for people
who do their
best to under-
stand you

for dogs
who do like the
smell of our
breath

for kids
who fall asleep
on your
lap

for water

for
daily miracles

for the
funny design
of rabbits

# library

The Library is home to your intuition. You can ask this inner knowing for advice when you have a problem. Give him or her a beautiful room because your intuition is an incredibly fast form of logic who always has a very interesting outlook on things. It might not always be right, but it's always worth listening to. The more you listen, the clearer and purer the voice will become.

This voice can be difficult to hear sometimes. So in this Library everything is kept in alphabetical order in large brown leather-bound books, because for some strange reason you believe what you already know once it's written down. So imagine yourself in the middle of all those books—with your eyes closed. Take a few deep breaths and think of what it is you want clarity in, the problem that you need answered. Keep both feet firmly on the ground and try to think with your body instead of your head. How do your legs feel, are they light or heavy? How does your belly feel, spacious or tight? How are your chest and your breathing, free or dejected? How about your throat, open or squeezed shut? And your jaws, loose or clenched? After scanning your body, you'll know how you feel about the situation at hand. Now ask the books around you to come up with the words you need to describe this feeling. See what words turn up. If your body is unable to help you any further in finding the right answer, you could always ask other people.

A Library in your Castle in the Clouds can be used to corral your intuition into helping you find solutions to problems. By the simple choice of asking this advisor, you will know where a solution can be found.

If you had a problem, who would you ask for advice?

# cloakroom

The Cloakroom is one big fancy costume
party that enables you to look at yourself in
different ways. Design a beautiful space and
then start by picking the T-shirt of the day.

## AFFIRMATEES

There are T-shirts on a rack in your Castle in the Clouds—printed T-shirts with messages on them. These types of T-shirts are often worn to show what you enjoy. And what if that is you? If you wear one of these T-shirts in your Castle, you can be sure you will start to feel that way. Which T-shirt would you pick today? And how would it feel if you wear a T-shirt like that in daily life?

I trust me, all the way
I feel so easy
I am radiantly healthy
I am the sunshine of my life
I love my smiling face
I glow with the flow
I love me.
My god loves you too

## TRICK COSTUME

Imagine a wardrobe full of outfits that give you a special talent: golf gear that lets you putt like Tiger Woods, a stunning pair of wings that will enable you to fly, simple red underpants that give you courage—because it's red touching your sacrum where your spine begins. There's also sport shoes with air in them that really make you walk and feel lighter. A hand-knitted cardigan makes you soft. Put on the bear fur hat, and you can growl. Red high heels transform you into a self-assured vamp. Don the floral dress, and you are one with nature. A long raincoat protects you from critical looks. A T-shirt makes it summer. Slippers instantly make you calm and content with what you have. With the stunning ring you are hot marriage material, a ballet outfit and you are lithe and supple. Which outfits would you try on? Which ones would you like to own?

Which costumes would you like to use?

wearing these pearls makes you elegant and gracious

In this dress you will feel like a Princess

wear this vest, and you will be instantly soft

everybody wants your opinion when you have these glasses on

wearing these boots will make you the best country music singer whether you like it or not

you wouldn't think so, but with these shoes you can dance to any type of music

 STRENGTH

red underwear gives you strength, courage, and passion (when worn)

 CALM

blue underpants keep you calm and dignified

orange underwear gives you a sense of bliss

 FUN

FREEDOM

 a green set of underwear will give you a sense of harmony and freedom

IMAGINATION

yellow underpants strengthen your will

this violet beanie stimulates your spirituality

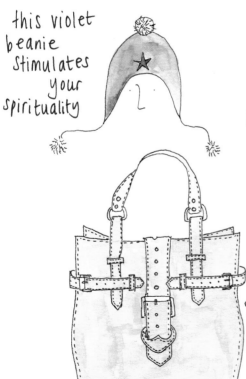

 wear this scarf and you're incredible with words, even at public speaking

stick these eyelashes on and you can flirt like the best of them.

with this nail polish on your toes it is impossible to get you off balance

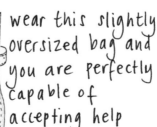

wearing these gloves will make you good at delegating

wear this slightly oversized bag and you are perfectly capable of accepting help

 wear this bracelet and you are the em-bodiment of peace

## A MIRRORED MIRROR

This mirror makes it impossible for you to look at your body in a critical way for a change. This time your body will be inspecting you. What will your body tell you when it looks at you? Does it also look at every little blemish in your character? Does it punish you as hard? Or is your body much kinder to you than you are to it? Is your body begging for a less critical look? It works so hard, keeping you healthy, fighting germs. Is your body begging for food, exercise, space, air?

## THE PERFECTLY CUT HUMAN MIRROR

We often use other people as a mirror. A simple example: you make a joke, other people laugh, you think you're funny. If they don't laugh, it could make you think you are not funny. You are inclined to relate your self-image to the reaction and reflection of others.

If you were to look in a mirror and see yourself really long and stretched out, you would assume there's something wrong with the mirror and not your self-image. Using people as a mirror might mean you are looking into a faulty mirror. They could be too busy at that moment in time, not at all interested, in a totally different headspace, having completely different "connotations," envious, or not capable of recognizing what you are doing. You're projecting in a faulty mirror, and you could get angry or disappointed in your own image (that would be you) as a result.

Try looking into a "perfectly cut human mirror." Let's face it, people have not been put on this earth to serve as a mirror for you. But since you use them for that purpose regularly, do it right this time. The perfectly cut human mirror comes in different models. What does the ideal father mirror see when he looks at you? Ideal in the way that he takes all the time in the world to look at you, all the space, warm feelings, as an adult unhindered by the past. He has the opportunity to see all of you. What does he see? What does he reflect to you? Are you happy with that? Do you radiate enough in real life to expect a reflection like that? Look into all these different mirrors. Give the ones you like a permanent place in your Castle in the Clouds.

What does the ideal father, mother, brother, sister, employer, employee, friend, husband, wife, daughter, son, teacher, coach see when he/she looks at you?

> The Cloakroom in your Castle in the Clouds can make you see yourself in different ways from all angles.

perfect mother

ideal father

perfect boss

perfect lover

perfect sister

best brother

loveliest animal.
ha they are always
perfect. that's
why they can give us
so much love.

how would a perfect
(= warm, kind, wise)
you look at yourself?

It is almost impossible to use people as a mirror to get a true image of yourself. But since you are doing it often if not all the time, think about what would happen if that human mirror is perfectly cut. What would you see if you look at yourself from the point of view of the perfect father and these other ideal people. (Perfect meaning that they are calm, wise, open, loving and totally into you.)

# royal suite of evil

Every person knows good and evil. Every person is good and evil. The choice you have is whether you want to feed your evil side and thoughts and make them stronger, or do you ignore them effortlessly. Ignoring is not the same as denial; anything you persistently deny will jump on your neck from a dark alley one fine day.

The best way to deal with your evil side is to acknowledge it and to give it lots of space in a superdeluxe royal hotel suite. Make it so comfortable that it doesn't even want to come out and manifest itself. So that it hangs around in its suite getting slow and a little pudgy, sometimes unwashed and often not even dressed, gorging itself on the minibar and lazy from ordering room service.

It's good to know where your evil side is for two reasons: If you know it's neatly tucked away in room 13, it can't be anywhere else. And you know where to find it at times when you can use its fearless courage and borderless energy to let loose during an anger attack.

Being angry isn't so hard. Becoming angry, that's something different. Becoming angry is scary because it can change the atmosphere or ruin a relationship. So it seems easier to keep the peace and hold back— if only that worked. Anger can't really be held back, it oozes out on all sides: by sighing or avoiding eye contact, by saying; "I'll do it" with a martyr's smile, by not accepting help, by sabotaging someone else's spontaneity and joy, by gossiping, by refusing to forgive, by being mean, by threats (you're not invited to my party).

Maybe anger wouldn't have to work its way around all those hairpin bends if it were allowed to exist—if it didn't have to be shushed, tempered, or controlled. You can visualize it in this suite. Here it is allowed to be in all its glory.

## IN THE MINIBAR

You can keep your anger alive by feeding it the little bottles from the minibar. All you have to do is choose and name the right "poison." The pure essences are in those bottles, undiluted with a high percentage of anger. All twisted expressions of anger are disguised as innocent mixes and cocktails. The minibar has a few basic anger essences. For specific personal ones, you're going to have to call room service.

Like anger by disappointment: you didn't get what you had hoped or wished for (a promotion, attention, a compliment, a new look at the hairdressers, to be truly seen).

Anger from being powerless: things happen that you have no control over or think to have no control over (kids are annoying, neighbors are noisy, bills just keep coming in).

Anger as camouflage: better anger expressed than sadness or hurt inside (often the case in typical adolescent anger).

Anger from fear: a technique to attack in order to avoid rejection or possible embarrassment. A false self-defense so to speak, since you might not really be under attack. And if you are, it's better to become angry out of protection.

Anger from love: when there's injustice aimed at people, animals, things you love and care for.

Anger from protection: all that is yours or is a part of you, that is your garden, but also your principles, your integrity, and your body, these are boundaries that should not be crossed. It makes you angry when that happens—or you should become angry.

Next time you're angry, go to the minibar, pick the matching drink, and experience the pure anger. Anger is a good sign too: it shows you care about things and that they don't leave you untouched.

Sometimes being angry is not enough, you have to become angry. Such as when you have been cheated or someone has crossed your boundaries. But becoming angry is tricky. The dosage is the key: Am I overdoing it or has the message not hit yet—not too much and not too little? What do you want to achieve? Do you want to be right, do you want revenge, or do you just want to show your displeasure?

To become angry well is an art. There are four anger managers in your Castle in the Clouds who can help you. You can use them strategically and let them do the dirty work. There's a course by the Anger Managers on the pay-TV channel of the hotel. Show it to your own bad side. It might learn something.

| camouflage | fear | powerlessness | protection | love |

What's the root of your evil? What's the essence of your anger? Pick your poison.

# THE ANGER MANAGERS

## THE COACH

The coach is an absolute professional. He is capable of playing the ball and not the person in every situation. No matter how livid he is, he gets angry without apology or accusing someone. He'll just charge the situation. And then he can be merciless. You will never hear him say: "I'm sorry, but I think it's ridiculous that you're not paying attention because you feel the need to chat with your girlfriend on the phone instead" because none of it is relevant. What he would say from the bottom of his heart: "It sucks that that vase is broken, it makes me extremely angry." After venting his anger, he is always relieved, and he never adds extra fuel to the fire. The other party can apologize out of its own free will if that is called for. But because the other party wasn't attacked, there is no need for defense or a counterattack. It's beautiful to see.

## THE PURIST

The purist only mentions the feelings that come up with the event: how she feels. So she wouldn't say: "How stupid of you to drop and break that vase," but instead: "That vase meant a lot to me, and because you never mentioned you broke it, I get the feeling you don't value me."

This gives the other party a chance to explain that love for a vase and love for a person are two totally different types of love not to be mixed up.

The purist way doesn't always work. It can also be a rather sneaky way to accuse somebody—and if that is the idea, it won't go very well. For real emotional issues you can choose the purist, the pure purist. At work she would be a bit on the soft side (depending on the work you do of course).

## THE FRIDGE

The fridge keeps quiet for a long time. He uses that time to think, swallow, compare, abstract, and unite all of it in one haughty, indisputable, deadly argument—which may or may not be expressed. This is a very classy strategy, and it asks for a lot of stamina because the lack of reaction can cause the other party to think that he swallows everything. You have to be able to handle that. Don't let the other lure you into a reaction unless you have thought out the whole argument.

## THE FLORIST

The florist lets it all happen—reasonable and unreasonable, mean, low, emotional, the lot. She screeches, shouts, and yells. She accuses and apologizes and doesn't stop until everything that has happened, been felt, the contexts and all the possible consequences have been said and screamed in all possible tones, colors, and languages. In the end she usually has something to apologize for, and that's why she is called the florist. Don't hire the florist too often, only occasionally in dead-end relationships. Her consultation will either break or make them, so in either case things will be better than they ever were before.

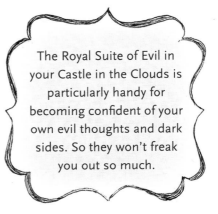

The Royal Suite of Evil in your Castle in the Clouds is particularly handy for becoming confident of your own evil thoughts and dark sides. So they won't freak you out so much.

# cinema della memoria

You could build a small private cinema in your Castle in the Clouds with a large screen and three rows of huge, comfortable, red velvet armchairs. Seat yourself front and center, and if you feel like it, you can invite other people to join you, but practice on your own first.

There's a little hatch above your head for the projector. A magical remote control is in your hand. The special thing about the cinema in your Castle in the Clouds is that you can look ahead and back on your own life. You can also erase scenes and rerecord them.

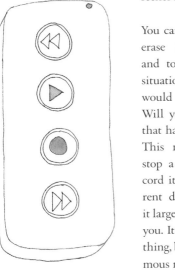

You can use the cinema to erase horrible memories and to imagine the ideal situation instead. How would you have liked it? Will you be able to make that happen in the future? This remote control can stop a bad memory, rerecord it, and give it a different direction. Experience it larger than life in front of you. It doesn't change anything, but it gives you enormous mental strength. Can you imagine the person costarring in this memory watching it with you? That you are showing how you would have liked it to be? What would his/her reaction be? Which part of the past will you take into your future? Which memory will you erase forever? Which memories and events make you who you are?

You can use the cinema to prepare for reality. You can learn certain skills with greater ease if you imagine them in advance. Don't look at the images on how you could have negative thoughts about a situation, but on how you want it to go. How does it look? How do you look? How does it smell?

You can use the cinema to determine your future. Not like a fortune-telling definer of fate, but more like a navigator or a psychic GPS. Experience your future on the big screen in 3D. What are the seven trailers for the complete box set of your life starting from now like? How does every aspect grow from now on?

## SEVEN FUTURE SCENARIOS DVD'S
Order the whole set!
– Home
– Work
– Love
– Family and friends
– Creative self-expression
– Leisure & fun
– Personal growth

How do you make sure that you play the lead in your own life?

## COMMERCIAL BREAK

What would a commercial for you look like? Make one for yourself as a friend, as a child, as a parent, as a lover, as a professional in your field of expertise. What are your USPs (unique selling points)? Can you think of a slogan for yourself?

## NEW MEMORIES

You make your own memories—often influenced by the way they are talked about. Your first memories can be shaped completely by your parents' stories. You've been told countless times how you fell in the water, learned to ride a bike, the funny words you used to say, so often that it created images that are stuck in your head. Just like the real thing. They may even have photographs to go with them so you can tell the stories in exactly the same way even though you may have been too young to really remember it.

There are also memories between friends, which get brought up a lot. Two different memories can continue on as one and be relived in your head.

Since it's possible to renew memories later on, it should also be possible to implant complete new memories into your head. Every word is a seed. When you read the word apple, a green, red, or yellow spherical thing with a stem appears in your head.

Here are five ideal scripts you can own as proper memories. Pick your favorite and repeat it several times. Give the memory time to adapt until it is accepted as with a transplant.

## IDEAL SCRIPTS FOR UNIVERSAL MEMORIES

### SCENE 1.
### INT. DAY. YOUR PARENTS' BEDROOM

You are six years old. You wake up in your own bed and you kind of sleepwalk toward your parents bedroom. With your eyes closed, you stroke your fingers along the wall, and you can feel its granular structure piercing your fingers. It hurts a little, but as soon as you take your fingers off, the pain is gone. Your feet are warm and plump, your pajamas are soft and have the sweet smell of sleep. You could wake up completely if you had to, but you'll snooze on quietly if you may. Your parents are awake because you can hear gentle cheerful voices. The bedroom is lit by a beam of sunlight streaming in through the curtains. Your mom has a beaming smile, throws the covers open, and pulls you in and over, straight into the middle of bed in between mom and dad. You dive under the covers. Your dad leans on one elbow, gently rests his chin on your head and whispers in your ear: "Hey little one, so you're back?" You're wedged between your parents like a piece of cheese between two slices of bread. Your face against the soft side of your mom and your back against the safe and solid chest of your dad. Your mom kisses your hair. Your parents continue to chat with each other and absentmindedly stroke and tickle you like a cat on one's lap. You open your eyes slowly and peek through your lashes. The sun stings your eyes a bit, and all you can see is the soft contours of your mom's and dad's faces. You are awake.

## SCENE 2.
## EXT. DAY. BUS STOP

You are fourteen years old. You are waiting at the bus stop with your very best friend. You chat about everything that happened at school that day. A man approaches. You both vaguely know him. He nods and joins you in waiting, which stops the conversation. The man coughs, and this is your cue to start laughing uncontrollably. When you look at each other, you need to laugh even harder. If you look the other way and you can only hear the other one, it makes you laugh even more. The tears are running down your cheeks. The man looks at you a little perturbed, all the more reason to laugh harder since you are meant to stop laughing. The bus stops, and you manage to calm down for a bit. You get on the bus and sit next to each other opposite two other people. Everybody is quiet and looking ahead inconspicuously. That's enough to set you off again, and you burst out with laughter. What sex does for beloveds, laughter does for friends. You feel an incredible bond, because nobody can see what the two of you see and hear together. Laughter is a release too; there is no room for other thoughts while laughing. Laughing consumes the now completely. You leave the bus in stitches. Laughing all the way home, where you burst out again when you have to talk to a brother, sister, nanny, neighbor, or mother. Nobody seems to understand you. That makes the bond and also the necessity of friendship even greater.

## SCENE 3.
## EXT. DAY. THE EMBANKMENT

You are seventeen years old. For weeks tension has been building between you and a boy (or a girl if you want) from your mutual circle of friends, a large group of boys and girls who spend their summer holidays together. Today is a languid summer's day. You're hanging out under the bridge at the embankment. The boys are looking cool on the bridge. Swimming trunks are low on their hips. Occasionally somebody jumps off the railing into the water. The girls are sunbathing on the embankment. They are chatting and looking up at the boys against the sunlight.

Every time you look his way, he looks back at you and vice versa—straight into each other's eyes, followed by a languid smile. Even if you didn't want to laugh, your eyes start to twinkle and the corners of your mouth only want to curl up. You bite your lip a bit, but the flaring of your nostrils gives it away. Fate is irreversible. Today you will kiss each other for the first time—which will make you an item. You are sure. It doesn't need to be expressed.

You jump off the bridge hand in hand. You have to let go of him for a nanosecond when you hit the water, but you find each other again straightaway. Your faces are really close together, and if it wasn't for a friend landing next to you with a big splash, you would have kissed. Not yet. But it's going to happen. The sun dries you, and you're all standing on the bridge a little bit later that afternoon. The T-shirts are back on. An ice-cold can, sparkling and cool against your warm lips. You are leaning against the bridge, and the little hairs on your arms touch. His friends are calling him, and he laughs a generous laugh. He stays right there. Today is the day. That's for sure.

## SCENE 4.
## INT. DAY. CAR

You are twenty-eight years old. You are head over heels in love, and the feeling is mutual. Because of work, you haven't been able to see each other for three weeks, and you are on your way to see him (or her) in a rental. It's a full day's drive. You've been on the road for a while when twilight sets in. You feel deeply happy. You are on your way to see your beloved. Your car zooms on, and your favorite radio station loses transmission. You are looking for a new station. They are playing old hits, and different memories flash past. The car's interior is all pale beige. There are little airholes in a vertical strip in the seating. You have to move once in a while to stop your clothes from sticking to the front seat.

You are starting to get hungry, and you stop by a road side restaurant. You cruise into the parking lot, and the flashing red neon sign reflects on the hood of your car. The waitresses inside have little cowboy hats dangling down their backs. You pick the hard way, and rather than sitting in a cozy corner booth in between thefamilies, you take a spot at the bar among the truckers in bright neon light. The give you a strange look,

but due to your irresistible glow, they leave you alone. An old crooked cowboy with a tanned face in jeans and a jean jacket walks past you, tips his hat, and says; "Tell him he's a lucky guy!" and leaves the restaurant. You pay the bill and continue your drive.

You find a rock station and sing out loud. When a car with whooping boys keeps driving next to you, you give them a friendly wave. When you cross from one state into the next, you sound your horn. A boy sticks his tongue out at you, and you stick yours out to him. You're going through the radio stations again and get stuck on a gooey country and western station. You sing along with long wails. You want to keep going and not stop until you get there. But you have to stop to go to the bathroom and get a  quick bite to eat and a drink. In the bathroom you throw some cold water on your face and brush your hair. Somebody wrote "love sucks" on the wall. With your eyeliner pencil you write "not for me" underneath.

Only two more hours to drive, you can do that without stopping. Then you'll be together again.

## SCENE 5.
## EXT. DAY. ORCHARD

You are seventy-four years old. Your spouse is a similar age. You are sitting in the orchard together. There's a kettle of water boiling on an open fire. You are sitting on a sturdy wooden crate. The summer is coming to an end. The trees are changing into all sorts of different colors, and the weather is getting cooler. You are wearing a large comfortable woolen cardigan. Your hands are in your lap. Your husband (or wife) throws some tea in the boiling water and pours you a mug. When he hands you the mug, his warm hands touch yours. Your eyes lock, and in them you see a mildness and comfort that has come with the years. You are content.

The Cinema della Memoria in your Castle in the Clouds is an exercise in taking control of your memories. You can't change what has happened, but you can change the way you look at it, even later on—and how you want it or do not want it to influence your life.

# royal stables

A horse is the best mode of transport there is. It gets you from A to B while with each step it brings you closer to yourself at the same time. This is why your Castle in the Clouds should have generous Royal Stables overlooking beautiful, outstretched, slanting green pastures. The horses can come and go as they please and make their own choice if they want to hang out with you or not. The Stables in your Castle in the Clouds can just as easily be on the second floor. If you look at the floors as a metaphor, contact with horses is one of the highest tests.

Horses can sense when a fly is planning to land on them. It is of vital importance for them to be able to feel what the other feels, wants, thinks, does, and thinks it wants to do. They literally catch everything you send out. To be able to handle horses, you have to correspond with them. You don't have to be strong, or happy, or not scared; none of that matters. They don't judge, but they don't know what to do with indistinctness—like acting cool when you are scared or acting strict when you actually feel sorry for them. Then they don't understand you or trust you, and it will be hard to get them to do something out of their own free will.

To be in balance, in tune with each other, you have to have your full attention in the now.

Horses read your entire being. When you interact with them, you have to have the same picture in your head and heart as you are projecting with your body. That is higher education for you. For us humans, that is. Not for horses, to them it's natural.

To start you could try and copy their being. The natural state of a horse is to think nothing and to feel everything. Sort of the exact opposite from humans (feel nothing and think everything). Okay, not all humans, just the gray ones in offices, stressed people, stupid people with whom regrettably we have quite a lot in common with. You shift from mental perception to sensory perception.

Stand up straight with both feet firmly on the ground—extra firm because it would be better if you had four legs. Take a slow and deep breath. Your flanks move back and forth, they expand when you breathe in and slowly move back in when you exhale. Your heartbeat is calm, and you carry your heart straight forward, your head is held high, almost in the clouds.

A noble posture. Meanwhile you feel your hairs in the wind, you can smell the sun on the leaves (or the newspaper, the kitchen table, the dashboard of your car), you can taste the thickness of the air, and all you see with your eyes is movement, of clouds, people. Your senses are on full blast, but you think nothing of it. No: "Oh such beautiful clouds and that aftershave is way too heavy, I think it might start to rain soon." You feel and register. No more.

Even if you don't want to have anything to do with horses, you can use them as test material to see if you are on the right path. Horses as a type of overall mirror.

A horse reflects your thoughts, your posture, your body, your heart, your head, and your intentions, all at the same time.

So you can walk around in your Royal Stables and scan your own body. Is your body switched on and your head switched off? Is your belly soft, your eyes soft and alert, your shoulders low and strong, loose jaws, spacious chest, legs heavy, and feet warm and stuck to the ground? If that is the case, the castle horses will come up to you to be with you (with a gate between you if you prefer).

If you do want to do a bit more with the horses, you can communicate with the castle horses via your belly—as if you swallowed the remote control. In your belly you can bundle your energy into a ball if you want them to keep their distance and respect your space. You can soften your belly if you want them to approach. It works with people too, but horses are more sensitive and unambiguous in their reaction.

When you walk through the Royal Stables, which horse would approach you today?

## 1. THE COOL HORSE

The cool horse, "you can trust me," is a very big and calm horse. You feel like a little kid with dangling legs when you're on its back. The cool horse takes the lead and is very careful with you. He trots calmly and shows you the whole world. But if you start to interfere and tell him what he should or shouldn't do, all his strength will turn against you. So if you can have fun and surrender to him, the cool horse is the ideal horse for you.

If you admit honestly that you find horses big and scary without belittling yourself or apologizing, the cool horse will approach you in a friendly way.

## 2. THE SOFT HORSE

The soft horse, "I'll do anything you ask from me but that doesn't make us friends," is hypersensitive and fast as lightning. She moves at the slightest instruction as quick as an arrow. That's fun, but that's where the hidden danger is too. She'll do anything for you even if it damages her own health or goes past her own fears. The challenge therefore is not to get all sorts of thing done but to build up a friendship and a bond of trust. If you have the power to know where you end and the other begins, you have it in you to build a great friendship with her. If it gives you pleasure to think of the other to gain trust, then this is your horse. Together with you she can conquer the world.

If you have the patience to let things evolve in their own time and don't try to force or control a situation, the soft horse will approach you very carefully.

## 3. THE JOLLY HORSE

The jolly horse, "we are friends but that doesn't mean I'll do everything you ask," loves to put his big warm nose on your neck, knocks over the wheelbarrow, and undoes your coat. If you can manage to be a clear leader without overcompensating with aggression or going power mad, he will want to play with you with equal tenderness. If you become harsh and mean, you will be faced by a harsh and stubborn horse. He can teach you not to apologize for your strength and not to be ashamed of your clarity. If the boundaries are marked, the two of you are going to have a lot of fun. If you manage, or if you want to learn, to express your wishes with equal love as well as clarity, the jolly horse will curiously seek you out and surprise you with its good nature, enthusiasm, and openness.

## 4. THE DREAM HORSE

The dream horse, "I'll take you with me and return you in the morning," is a beautiful white horse with a long, soft, flowing mane. You'll dance together through the night and back. You are actually in between two worlds. Your dream horse is waiting for you as soon as you fall asleep. You only have to believe that it's true for it to be so.

If you need a horse that is with you in feeling, then the dream horse will come to you, as a totem or guardian angel.

## 5. THE FIRE HORSE

The fire horse, "I will give you all the strength and energy you need," is a fierce and fearless horse. If you can manage to get onto the same frequency, you can empower each other, and together you are invincible. You melt together into an inhuman and unhorse-like creature who can achieve anything it wants. If you are not afraid of your own power, the fire horse is a suitable friend for you.

If you possess an incredible energy and you feel like changing the world, the fire horse will come to you roaring, stomping its hooves on the ground, and rearing up in front of your nose. If you can manage to take a firm stand amid the roars and legs mowing through the air, he will recognize his equal and want to be with you.

## 6. THE PRIMAL HORSE

The primal horse, "I will not come to you, I will not walk away from you, but we can get anywhere together," can only be guided by intention and intuition. Bits and reins, saddles and spurs, and pretty steps and tricks are all nonsense. Being together in true unity is the only goal. Beyond fear for these awe-inspiring animals, beyond the gaining of trust, beyond the putting up of boundaries, beyond the honoring of beauty, and beyond the sparkling feeling of bundling powers is the primal horse, in all its simplicity—to be together with you in a timeless and goalless, but certainly not senseless way. There's a primal horse in every horse, so it could be a stage you can reach with any horse after you've spent a lot of time together.

If your only expectation from a horse is to form a new being together in whatever way it presents itself without preconceived expectations, the primal horse will come to you.

The Royal Stables in your Castle in the Clouds are a good forum to see if your body can guide your heart and head, that you correspond mentally, emotionally, and physically. Shift from a mental perception to a sensory perception with a horse as your guide.

# heart chamber

Seven hippies are squatting in your Heart Chamber.
They started a commune in your castle, and everybody is
welcome. The hippies give you permission to feel everything
that is humanly possible without attaching any consequences
to them or without you having to take any responsibility for
them. This means that in your Heart Chamber you are allowed
to let your heart overflow with love for someone who doesn't
love you back. In this room you are allowed to feel pain that
should have passed a long time ago. Here you are allowed to
feel what it's like to be rejected without having to keep it
together or ever having been rejected.

It's better if you don't try to resist the idea of hippies in your heart. These are beautiful, peace-loving, and gracious hippies. They are functioning very well indeed. Of course, squatting is against the law. But it's worthwhile to look the other way on this.

These seven hippies have managed to build up a harmonious life together. They know and respect each other's qualities, like mindfulness, joy, gratitude, compassion, authenticity, connectedness, and peace. There isn't one worth more or less than the other. There is no leader. There is enough space for everyone to shine and be present in all their glory.

They have catchy hippie names like Joy, Grace, Peace, and Sky. Don't bother trying to remember them though. You would run the risk of favoring one or getting too attached, and that could lead to you interfering with their business. They know what they are doing.

The hippies have a self-sufficient system and lead an autonomous life. There's a large open fire in the middle of the room which heats up the entire Castle in the Clouds. They have a vegetable garden outside which supplies their food—and clouds are turned into drinking water. A sheep gives its wool. The cow gives its milk. All that comes in is processed and used. All hippies work together as one unit.

The rest of the day is spent in a circle around the fire. They take turns throwing a log on, and they play a bit on their drums. Once in a while they receive visitors. Every feeling you experience could be imagined as a visitor to the Heart Chamber. Everybody is welcome and is offered a place on a cushion. "Have a seat and tell us your whole story." Everybody listens to each other's stories as if they are the most fascinating travel stories and experiences with endless attention and devotion and without sentiment or judgment. They have the quality to leave the story with the

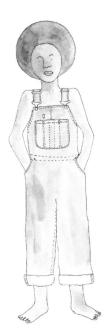

storyteller. They don't take on the drama. That's why all can feel free to tell their stories openly without any reservations. The hippies can experience every feeling without self-pity or overestimation.

A guest can talk about fear, jealousy, loneliness, or being passed by—about anything that can be felt. And all is well. It is heard and understood. When that's done, the guest is given a log to put on the fire. That's how the Castle in the Clouds remains warm.

If there are issues you need advice on, they are happy to give it to you. All together they make a democratic decision: "Go for it, fall in love, we will catch you if you fall again." They can because they aren't afraid of anything.

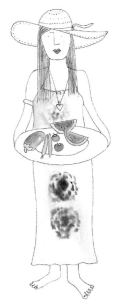

"Yeah, it feels good to go traveling. We don't know if you have the money to do it or if it's convenient right now, but we say GO!" or: "That real estate agent is a smooth talker. It just doesn't feel right to us. Don't do it." If you're not sure about how to listen to the hippies yet, you could try to listen to your body. Listen to their drums, to your heartbeat: Calm is usually a good sign, a clear rhythm too. When the stomach rumbles (not to be mistaken for hunger), shallow breaths, irregular heartbeat, and sweat are all signals from the hippies who are saying— not so good, don't do it. A steady and

Where have you been?
What do you remember?
Which place don't you want go back to?
Where would you still like to go?

loud heartbeat is preparing you for a big yes. Exciting, scary, thrilling, DO IT.

All people are welcome in your Heart Chamber, even those you have a problem with. Watch the hippies, see how they offer him or her, without distinction, a cushion, a cup of herbal tea, and a log. This person puts logs on the fire too and helps to heat your Castle.

If you don't listen to your heart, the hippies will retreat more and more. Society and all its conspiracies are what the hippies avoid, and they walk their march of protest in silence. They are pacifists. They pull back. They hibernate. They will beat their drums frantically from time to time to get your attention. You will feel a chill running down your spine from time to time because the fire isn't stirred up as high. But they will keep their mouths shut.

It's the same with your real heart. To enable it to speak, you have to listen to it. If you haven't done that for too long, it will stop talking. Done. And when the heart stops talking, the head has no guideline, and it starts working overtime. And what's funny is that it's the heart that will let you know when your head is doing overtime—with palpitations.

The day you decide to listen to the hippies again is a happy day. They are overjoyed and never hold a grudge. They can't wait to tell you all sorts of things, they stir up the fire, and the drums sound their deep regular beats.

The most important thing is that you just let the hippies do their thing. What does that leave for you,

what can you do? Not so much. Just trust the idea that they know what they are doing.

You don't want to regulate your heart. Tell it when to beat.

What it should or shouldn't feel. When it should feel. Don't try to give a name to every feeling, and don't try to control the priority or order. You don't want to judge if a feeling is right, wrong, just, adequate, useful, or wanted. Leave it to the hippies. They have the courage to feel it all, process it, and they keep it in the Heart Chamber.

The only influence you have is your breath. Your breath is your telephone line to your Heart Chamber. When you breathe slowly and deeply, the drums will beat a slower, more regular, and deeper rhythm, the rhythm of your heartbeat.

What should you do here? Not so much. You just have to feel extremely welcome. Have a cushion, a log, a cup of tea. Know that you are wanted and loved. Feel free to dance, cry, love, and to let your heart overflow with bliss.

You can try to imagine the guests and their stories. What's the story of Loneliness. What has he been through with you? And Feeling Left Out? And Jealousy? And Fear? And Hopelessness? And In Love? And Hopelessly in Love? And Excitement? And Passion? And Superiority? And Vengefulness? And Lethargy? And Indifference? And Sadness? And Great Fun? And All-Embracing Love?

Can you sit back, let the guests tell their stories, and watch how the hippies handle that with compassion without trying to own the stories? You don't have to learn from the hippies, because they will do it all for you. It is within you already, just butt out.

# tower room

The Tower Room is there just for you.
This is the place where you can be your ultimate optimal self.
What function should the room have? What is it that you feel
a need for? What do you want to do here? What does it look
like? Who is there with you? How does it feel? How does it
smell? What are you wearing? What colors do you see?
What is the view? What kind of furniture do you have there?
How big is the space? Who will be getting the key to
your Tower Room?

What furniture and objects would you like to put in your Tower Room?

# treasure
# chamber

In the Treasure Chamber of your Castle in the Clouds, you are able to feel ultimate gratitude. You are capable of enjoying and seeing the beauty in everything as soon as you step inside. The Treasure Chamber enables you to perceive everything as valuable, unique, worthy, and magical. You are calm, not excited, cheerful, la la la. It's more mindful, concentrated, and precise. It goes way beyond seeing obstacles as challenges, traumatic experiences as wise lessons, and glasses as half full (half full, come on!). That water is the transparent ink, the ink that is used on all invisible contracts that unite us all. That water is the purest tears, the tears of the gods that they shed for all the hurt in the world. That water is the pure essence of source, the source that originated all of life. No half full here.

You are in a permanent state of wonder and admiration, deeply rooted, as if beauty and dearness are the only truth. You feel wise. Your breathing is calm and regular. Admiration is felt without excitement or outward signs because you know that the source is inexhaustible. The corners of your mouth curl up of their own accord. Since you are the one discovering the beauty, it makes you the true treasure. Polish yourself up a bit more and admire yourself in that big golden mirror.

Can you visualize a room around you that only has beautiful things in it? What do you see?

A Treasure Chamber awakens the feeling of wanting to own: gold, diamonds, designer clothes, cars, flashy espresso machines, the prize booth of a big TV game show. Think about it. Enjoy it.

That was the fun part. Here comes the tricky part— which could turn into a far more rewarding part. But it might not feel like that initially.

It's easy to identify with possessions. If I have a fast car, people will perceive me as flashy. If I wear beautiful clothes, I'm successful. It appears to build self-esteem when we identify with things, matter, stuff—as with the people you associate with, the hobbies you have, the music you listen to, the films you saw first.

That seems easy, but it is exhausting, because you can't program another person's brain. You can't create a profile of yourself and regulate what others think. Everybody is free to think what they want. Who you are does not originate in other people's heads. Who you are is made by you, in your head and in your heart. You are who you want to be.

The good thing about your Castle in the Clouds is that there's no obligation to identify yourself; it's your right to de-identify.

If you identify with possessions, achievements, background, rituals, habits, music, hair color, appearance, and life phase, you can let go of all that, here in the Treasure Chamber. By stripping your "profile," you will get to the core of who you are. Knowing who you are is your most valuable possession. If you are in the right mood, you can see it as a pearl. That is what's left when you peel off all the sandy muck. It's like nuclear fission that gets more powerful the closer you get to the core, like a treasure you could be looking for a whole lifetime.

You are not the car you drive.
You are not your hair color.
You are not your height.
You are not your profession.
You are not your traumatic experience.
You are not your funny remarks.
You are not your achievements.
You are not your Facebook profile.
You are not your age.
You are not your favorite sports team.
You are not your fears.
You are not your house.
You are not your latest gadget.
You are not your thoughts.
You are not your circle of friends.
You are not your family.
You are not your parents.
You are not your children.
You are not your weight.
You are not your favorite drink.

In some cases it can be a relief to de-identify, and in some cases it can make you feel naked and bare. It's a type of mental streaking. What remains when you take everything off?

You are the biggest treasure. But who are you? What are you? What is your purpose in life? The reason to get up in the morning? Or like the Japanese say so beautifully, your ikigai?

To find out, you could make a personal Treasure Map. The different rooms in your Castle in the Clouds will provide you with keys. You may need them all, maybe only a couple, or you might need other rooms and keys. Maybe there are rooms that are important to you now, and other rooms will be in different phases of your life or moods. Your Castle in the Clouds is an opportunity to make the inside of your head your favorite place to be. It is a way to start to look at yourself in a different way, from a new perspective, where you can approach yourself mildly.

Maybe you have been circling around your treasure for a while. You might have had an inkling of an idea of what's hidden in your treasure chest, but you may need the rest of your life to feel it and put it into words. That's what life is for.

You are your potential.
You are your wish.
You are your soul and inspiration.

Try to find out who you are by choosing
your own path on the Treasure Map. How could the rooms in
your Castle in the Clouds be of help? To get to know yourself better,
you could express your desires for example (Garden of Wishes), conquer
your fears (Inner Courtyard), recognize your limiting thoughts (Mental Spa),
be shamelessly proud of yourself (Salon), regulate the stream of information
(Kitchen), allow your sadness (Hall of Tears), have the courage to trust your
heart (Heart Chamber), fight your embarrassment (Suite of Shame),
acknowledge your anger (Royal Suite of Evil), disengage from your past
(Cinema della Memoria), deflate your ego (Small Chapel of the Soul),
disengage the automatic pilot from your thinking (Head Office),
It sounds like a lot. You could suffice by wishing. What would you
like to find in your treasure chest? What would you like your
essence to be? What would you like your purpose
in life to be?

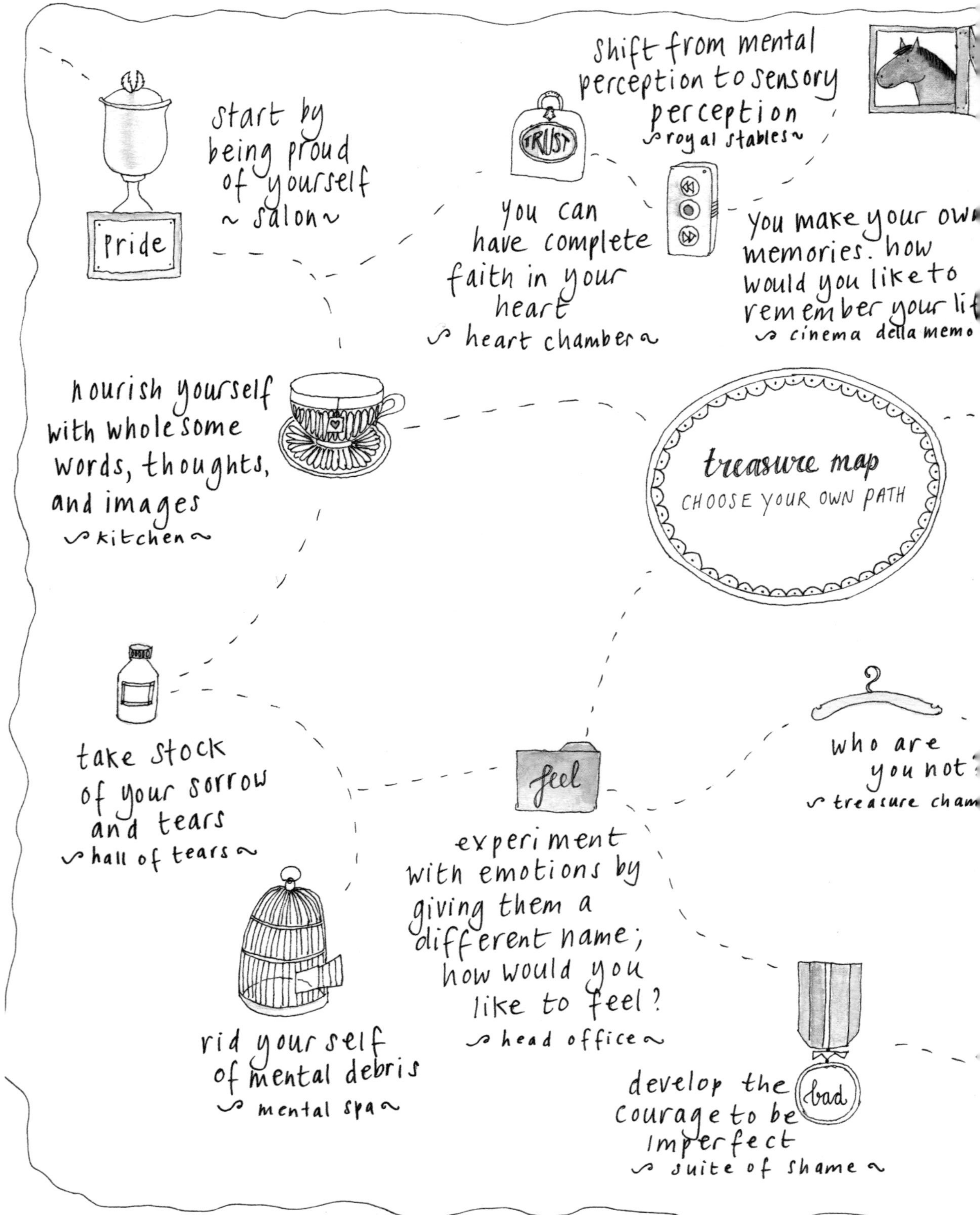

start by
being proud
of yourself
~ salon ~

shift from mental
perception to sensory
perception
~ royal stables ~

**Pride**

**TRUST**

you can
have complete
faith in your
heart
~ heart chamber ~

you make your own
memories. how
would you like to
remember your lif
~ cinema della memo

nourish yourself
with wholesome
words, thoughts,
and images
~ kitchen ~

*treasure map*
CHOOSE YOUR OWN PATH

who are
you not
~ treasure cham

take stock
of your sorrow
and tears
~ hall of tears ~

**feel**

experiment
with emotions by
giving them a
different name;
how would you
like to feel?
~ head office ~

rid yourself
of mental debris
~ mental spa ~

**bad**

develop the
courage to be
imperfect
~ suite of shame ~

listen to your intuition
~ library ~

who are you capable of being?
~ cloakroom ~

slay the dragons who stand between you and your wishes
~ garden of wishes ~

you are your angry and mad side too
~ royal suite of evil ~

HELLO my name is

accept every personality within you by throwing them a party
~ ballroom ~

become aware of your ego, where it is helpful and where it pinches
~ small chapel for your soul ~

what makes you happy?
~ hall of happiness ~

chateau miraval

have the courage to believe in the result without doubting the creative process
~ gallery ~

who were you? how much of who you once were is still there?
~ playroom ~

have the courage to begin the creative process without thinking of the result
~ art studio ~

defend your inner courtyard; learn to protect yourself
~ inner courtyard ~

## ABOUT THE AUTHOR

Barbara Tammes started her career as a copywriter in the mid-1980s, at age nineteen. She has worked as a designer and creative director for major international advertising agencies in Amsterdam, London, Milan, and Cape Town, and her work has won numerous prestigious awards worldwide.

In 2000 Barbara became an independent creative, teaming up with The Mind, a New York-based online think tank, working for different Dutch "green" companies. She lives on a farm outside Amsterdam with her husband, two kids, five horses, two dogs, some cats, and a barn owl. Visit her at www.barbaratammes.com.